A Guide to
Mathematics
Leadership

A Guide to
Mathematics
Leadership

Sequencing
Instructional
Change

Don S. Balka | Ted H. Hull | Ruth Harbin Miles

CORWIN
A SAGE Company

For information:

Corwin
A SAGE Company
2455 Teller Road
Thousand Oaks, California 91320
(800) 233-9936
Fax: (800) 417-2466
www.corwinpress.com

SAGE Pvt. Ltd.
B 1/I 1 Mohan Cooperative
  Industrial Area
Mathura Road, New Delhi 110 044
India

SAGE Ltd.
1 Oliver's Yard
55 City Road
London EC1Y 1SP
United Kingdom

SAGE Asia-Pacific
  Pte. Ltd.
33 Pekin Street #02-01
Far East Square
Singapore 048763

Printed in the United States of America

Library of Congress Cataloging-in-Publication Data

Balka, Don.
A guide to mathematics leadership: sequencing instructional change/Don S. Balka, Ted H. Hull, Ruth Harbin Miles.
      p. cm.
Includes bibliographical references and index.
ISBN 978-1-4129-7543-8 (pbk.)
    1. Mathematics—Study and teaching. 2. Educational leadership. I. Hull, Ted H. II. Miles, Ruth Harbin. III. Title.

QA11.2.B34 2010
510.71—dc22   2009031802

This book is printed on acid-free paper.

09   10   11   12   13   10   9   8   7   6   5   4   3   2   1

Acquisitions Editor:	Cathy Hernandez
Editorial Assistant:	Sarah Bartlett
Production Editor:	Veronica Stapleton
Copy Editor:	Nancy Conger
Typesetter:	C&M Digitals (P) Ltd.
Proofreader:	Jennifer Gritt
Indexer:	Sheila Bodell
Cover Designer:	Rose Storey
Graphic Designer:	Scott Van Atta

Contents

List of Figures

Preface

This book is for leaders responsible for improving the mathematics achievement of students. The process presented in the following pages will be useful to leaders who want their teachers, grade levels, departments, schools, and districts to successfully build a high-quality mathematics program based upon the five principles identified by the National Council of Teachers of Mathematics (NCTM; 2000): equity, curriculum, teaching, learning, and assessment, as well as the four leadership principles identified by the National Council of Supervisors of Mathematics in the *PRIME Leadership Framework* (NCSM; 2008): equity leadership, teaching and learning leadership, curriculum leadership, and assessment leadership.

To facilitate leaders' actions toward positive change, we present in this book a developmental, sequential process, which is shown in Figure 0.1, Outline of Developmental Stages. While the process unfolds over many months and is long term by nature, we also show mathematics leaders how to effectively focus their time and energy so as to achieve shorter-term goals and objectives. Leaders will find guidance for change initiatives that are small enough to manage, yet large enough to matter. We have incorporated NCTM Principles and NCSM Leadership Principles throughout each stage of the process and offer recommendations that are logical, supported by research, and easy to follow. Suggestions for targeting equity are also provided in discussion of each stage of the model.

The improvement process we describe begins with refining, honing, aligning, and implementing the mathematics curriculum. Curriculum improvement is critical to long-term success and student achievement. In addition, the curriculum is a recognized part of the leader's sphere of influence. Initiating improvement within the mathematics curriculum does not require permission to purchase new programs, to adjust schedules, or to seek outside resources. Mathematics leaders need only to make the decision to begin.

Figure 0.1 Outline of Developmental Stages

Goal: Engaging and Empowering Staff

Leadership Goal: The mathematics leader ensures that processes are in place to empower and engage staff.

A mathematics leader guarantees that:

- Staff is included in decision making.
- Communication structures are in place.
- Dynamics of engagement and empowerment are understood.

Stages for Engaging

Developmental Stage: Articulating the Curriculum

The mathematics leader ensures that the school district, campus, or school has a clearly articulated mathematics curriculum.

A mathematics leader guarantees that:

- The curriculum is aligned to national, state, and local standards.
- All students are given the opportunity to learn appropriate content.
- The scope, sequence, and timeline align to the instructional year.
- The curriculum is rigorous.

Developmental Stage: Implementing the Curriculum

The mathematics leader ensures that the mathematics curriculum is implemented as designed.

A mathematics leader guarantees that:

- The developed curriculum plan is followed.
- Student progress is monitored via ongoing benchmark assessments.

Developmental Stage: Incorporating Effective Instructional Practices

The mathematics leader ensures that effective instructional practices are implemented.

A mathematics leader guarantees that:

- A variety of instructional strategies are used.
- Instructional materials match desired classroom instructional practices.
- Data are used to inform practice.

Stages for Empowering

Developmental Stage: Providing Timely and Targeted Feedback

The mathematics leader ensures that timely feedback concerning curriculum implementation and classroom strategies are provided to appropriate personnel.

A mathematics leader must guarantee that:

- Pertinent data are gathered and used to inform learning.
- Information is targeted to group or specific teacher needs.
- Trust is built throughout the staff.

(Continued)

> **Figure 0.1** (Continued)
>
> ### *Developmental Stage: Establishing Professional Learning Communities*
>
> The mathematics leader ensures that the professional learning communities are established with suitable organization and structure support.
>
> A mathematics leader guarantees that:
>
> - Staff is provided time to collaborate.
> - Staff operates as a professional learning community.
> - Staff is provided time to reflect upon teaching and learning.
>
> ### *Developmental Stage: Fostering Professional Development*
>
> The mathematics leader ensures that continuous professional development is provided. A mathematics leader guarantees that ideas about mathematical content, instruction, and assessment are relevant, sustained over time, emerge from identified teacher needs, and are directly related to classroom procedures.

The process presented here provides leaders with the guidance necessary to complete one entire improvement cycle—beginning with articulating a curriculum and ending with fostering professional development—while continually engaging and empowering mathematics teachers. Although improvement efforts are inevitably recursive in nature, completing even one improvement cycle can have a significant impact upon mathematics teaching and learning.

The audience for this book encompasses all those who are engaged in mathematics leadership, including K–12 mathematics curriculum specialists, principals, building specialists, department chairs, mentors, coaches, new and emerging leaders, and higher-education faculty who train leaders in mathematics education.

Although the book is geared toward mathematics leaders who have a background in mathematics content, we recognize that leaders lacking mathematical content expertise also provide oversight for mathematics programs. This book is intended to meet the needs of principals, curriculum directors, and assistant superintendents of curriculum and instruction who directly supervise mathematics leaders. And, although written as a guide for those in formal leadership positions, anyone involved in mathematics education will find the material beneficial.

NEED FOR LEADERSHIP

The need for informed, proactive leaders at all levels of mathematics education is crucial to ensuring equity and achieving success in implementing quality mathematics programs, in other words, reaching the high ideals of NCTM and NCSM. *Principles and Standards for School Mathematics* (NCTM, 2000) asserts "There is an urgent and growing need for mathematics teacher-leaders—specialists positioned between classroom teachers and administrators who can assist with the improvement of mathematics education" (p. 375). In addition, there is an urgent need for leadership in mathematics at the principal and district-office levels. Although leadership and professional development are key points in the mission statement, resources for identifying, guiding, and training new, emerging, or existing leaders are difficult to find (NCSM, 2008).

While there are numerous generic resources that suggest actions, strategies, and approaches for educational leaders, resources demonstrating how mathematics leaders can successfully realize NCTM principles and achieve a high-quality mathematics program are scarce (NCSM, 2008). Those that do exist are often not organized sequentially, nor do they embed the recommendations into an on-going plan for improvement. This lack of sequential organization poses problems for leaders. Leaders need more than the lists of isolated, disconnected recommendations found in many resources and state documents. While lists of recommendations can serve as checklists or self-assessments, two questions still remain for mathematics leaders: *Where do I start?* and *What do I do next?*

This guide answers those questions. We begin by identifying from research the knowledge and skills mathematics instructional leaders need in order to have the greatest positive impact on student learning. We have clustered and organized the information so that as mathematics leaders progress through the book, each chapter provides the scaffolding and framework for the next chapter. As stages are presented, the principles are addressed, and leaders progress toward a comprehensive, high-quality mathematics program. A primary function of mathematics leaders is to translate the NCTM Principles into practical actions—actions that are also consistent with the NCSM Leadership Principles. The process presented here will help leaders achieve this goal.

OVERVIEW OF THE BOOK

This book is divided into three parts: Preparing the Foundation, A Leadership Model, and Continuing the Work.

Part I: Preparing the Foundation

Chapter 1, Understanding and Clarifying Leadership in Mathematics, explores the correlation between the process presented in this book and the recommendations of the National Council of Teachers of Mathematics and the National Council of Supervisors of Mathematics.

Mathematics leaders *engage* and *empower* staff in the art of teaching. The theory and research behind engaging and empowering individuals is identified in Chapter 2, appropriately titled Engaging and Empowering Staff. This theme is reinforced throughout the remainder of the book.

Part II: A Leadership Model

In Chapter 3, Articulating the Curriculum, leaders engage teachers by working to *articulate* mathematics content and materials, providing a foundation for success by identifying a reasonable and manageable scope, sequence, and timeline for instruction. This work of articulation is done *with* teachers, not *to* them.

Leaders continue to engage teachers by actually *implementing* the curriculum as designed through the processes outlined in Chapter 4, Implementing the Curriculum. Implementation, to be successful, is monitored. Monitoring occurs by having educators from all levels and roles actually enter classrooms. Educators use a customized classroom visit form that evaluates only the degree of program implementation, not the teachers.

Recognizing the hard work teachers do is important. Nonetheless, working hard is of little benefit if content is misaligned. And, teaching correct content in appropriate ways is no harder for teachers than teaching misaligned content in ineffective ways. Leaders must help ensure that teachers create horizontally and vertically aligned content. Leaders also work to help teachers develop assessments that align to content. Only when assessments align with content can teaching effectiveness be accurately evaluated. With aligned curriculum implementation underway, the focus of leaders shifts to supporting teachers by utilizing *effective practices,* as described in Chapter 5, Incorporating Effective Instructional Practices.

The process up to this point has leaders working to engage teachers in actually teaching what is to be taught, thus assuring adequate opportunity for students to learn. Leaders now shift their focus to empowering teachers by providing timely and targeted *feedback* (Chapter 6), establishing *professional learning communities* (Chapter 7), and fostering worthwhile *professional development* (Chapter 8).

Chapters 6, 7, and 8 discuss how to use meaningful data as a way to effectively analyze and reflect upon instructional and program effectiveness. Teachers and leaders need to have meaningful discussions about student progress. Ideally, these discussions are part of professional learning communities. The accuracy of data is a key to driving beneficial discussions that move beyond inclinations to express opinions about what works and what doesn't work. Without evidence, teachers will just as likely abandon effective practices as ineffective ones. Teachers and leaders need evidence to indicate whether something worked or not.

With the development of an articulated curriculum, implemented curriculum, effective strategies, and accurate data, teachers can engage in worthwhile and meaningful dialogues in professional learning communities. In some cases, leaders may have difficulty establishing professional learning communities due to budgetary concerns, scheduling concerns, or district-level concerns. For these reasons, we discuss establishing professional learning communities in Chapter 7 rather than at the beginning of the process. Mathematics leaders can do much to effectively engage and empower their staffs and can have tremendous, positive impact on student learning and achievement while working towards the long-term goal of establishing professional learning communities. If professional learning communities are thwarted, leaders can move forward to professional development (Chapter 8) that targets teachers' needs and is supported by data. By this time, a process will have been established to monitor the results of professional development and ensure that it has the desired impact.

Part III: Continuing the Work

Chapter 9 focuses on how students learn mathematics. Various tools help teachers facilitate students' ability to move from concrete stages to symbolic stages in mathematical learning. Active engagement is a key factor and involves student collaboration and making student thinking visible in the classroom.

The goal for leaders is to use their considerable influence to impact what happens in the mathematics classroom and to close the achievement gap. In working through the stages presented in this book, engaging and empowering staff members are critical features of that plan. Chapter 10 reminds leaders that the model presented here is cyclical. Continuous improvement of a mathematics program requires leaders to reevaluate over time.

ANSWERING LEADERSHIP QUESTIONS

The material in each chapter of this book asks and answers three important questions:

1. What is expected of mathematics leaders?

2. What are mathematics leaders to do?

3. What can mathematics leaders use?

The sections titled "What Are Leaders Expected to Do?" offer explanations of current research, providing a rationale and explanation for upcoming leadership actions. The "Leaders Ensure . . . " sections actually guide leaders through actions that achieve established expectations. The final sections, "Resources That Leaders Can Use," suggest additional recommended resources.

USING THE BOOK AS A GUIDE

As mentioned previously, the chapters in this book reflect a carefully ordered, sequential process that will lead to success in teaching and learning. Each chapter paves the way for the succeeding one—the knowledge, skills, and actions within the chapters overlap one to the next. With each stage, teachers and leaders become more actively engaged and more empowered. When the last stage, *Fostering Professional Development*, is reached, the entire process recycles at a richer and more fulfilling level as an engaged and empowered staff begins anew by reconsidering, reevaluating, and reforming a curriculum.

Leaders can use this book in a number of ways:

- to serve as a planning guide for school improvement efforts;
- to serve as a study guide for large or small groups;
- to serve as a reflective tool;
- to serve as a lens for focusing on areas needing improvement;
- to serve as a guide for developing new or future leaders; or
- to serve as a resource for verifying or comparing other resources.

Figure 0.1, Outline of Developmental Stages, may be used as a tool for leaders as they reflect upon the work of the school or district and evaluate where they have been and where they are going. The clarifying statements beneath each developmental stage can assist in maintaining a dual focus on both a long-term plan and short-term objectives.

Although some leaders may be tempted to skip a stage, each identified stage is crucial to student success in mathematics. Skipping a stage, such as developing an aligned curriculum, will ultimately undermine improvement efforts.

DEVELOPING FUTURE LEADERS

Current leaders can use this resource to develop and mentor new mathematics leaders who will understand and implement the principles identified by NCSM. The knowledge and skills discussed in the following pages are foundational for developing future leaders. As leaders use the book in a transparent, explicit, and inclusive manner, the training of future leaders is a tremendous by-product of their actions. Empowering and engaging staff members in the work of improving mathematics education builds invaluable leadership knowledge and skills. While undertaking this work with mathematics teachers, leaders will note that some teachers eagerly assume various supportive roles in the change initiatives. These teachers are likely to emerge as team leaders, department heads, or mathematics resource specialists in formal or informal ways. Some will become part of the leadership teams that help a district move toward the NCTM Principles and maintain such a focus in the future. In this way, the book serves a dual role for promoting leadership. First, it serves as a guide for current mathematics leaders, and second, by engaging and empowering staff in the improvement process, it provides the foundation that helps secure and foster future mathematics leaders.

The entire process is designed to instill hope for thousands of mathematics leaders and teachers working every day for betterment of their students. It can be done, and you can make it happen. In whatever way you choose to use this book, we encourage you to keep moving forward.

Acknowledgments

Corwin gratefully acknowledges the contributions of the following reviewers:

Angela T. Barlow, Associate Professor of Mathematics Education
University of Mississippi
Oxford, MS

D. Allan Brunner, Science/Mathematics Chair
Colton High School
Miles City, MT

Dr. Felicia Clark, Secondary Math Coordinator
LAUSD Local #8
Gardena, CA

Jenny Sue Flannagan, Director of Martinson Center for Math and
    Science
Regent University School of Education
Virginia Beach, CA

Lucia Flevares, Assistant Professor of Math
Ohio State University
Columbus, OH

Miriam S. Grosof, Professor Emeritus
Yeshiva University, Stern College for Women
New York, NY

Liz Marquez, Math Assessment Specialist
Educational Testing Services
Milltown, NJ

Kate Masarik, Assistant Professor
University of Wisconsin—Eau Claire
Eau Claire, WI

Edward Nolan, Math Department Chair
Albert Einstein High School
New Market, MD

Sherry Parrish, Math Specialist
South Shades Crest Elementary School
Hoover, AL

About the Authors

Don S. Balka, a former middle school and high school mathematics teacher, is Professor Emeritus in the Mathematics Department at Saint Mary's College, Notre Dame, Indiana. During his career as an educator, Don has presented over 2,000 workshops on the use of manipulatives with elementary and secondary students at national and regional conferences of the National Council of Teachers of Mathematics, state mathematics conferences, and at inservice trainings for school districts throughout the United States. In addition, he has taught classes in schools throughout the world, including Ireland, Scotland, England, Saudi Arabia, Italy, Greece, Japan, and the Mariana Islands in the South Pacific. Don has written over 20 books on the use of manipulatives for teaching K–12 mathematics, and is a coauthor of the Macmillan K–5 elementary mathematics series *Math Connects.* Don has served as director for the National Council of Teachers of Mathematics, the National Council of Supervisors of Mathematics, and the School Science and Mathematics Association. He lives with his wife, Sharon, in LaPaz, Indiana.

Ted H. Hull completed 32 years of service in public education before retiring and opening Hull Educational Consulting. He served as a mathematics teacher, K–12 mathematics coordinator, middle school principal, director of curriculum and instruction, and a project director for the Charles A. Dana Center at the University of Texas in Austin. While at the University of Texas, (2001 to 2005), he directed the research project "Transforming Schools: Moving From Low-Achieving to High-Performing Learning Communities." As part of the project, Ted worked directly with district leaders, school administrators, and teachers in Arkansas, Oklahoma, Louisiana, and Texas to develop instructional leadership skills and implement effective mathematics instruction. Ted is a regular presenter at local, state, and national meetings. He has written numerous articles for the NCSM newsletter including *Understanding the Six Steps of Implementation: Engagement by an Internal or External Facilitator* (2005) and *Leadership Equity: Moving Professional Development Into the Classroom* (2005), as well as *Manager to Instructional Leader* (2007) for the NCSM Journal of Mathematics Education Leadership. He has been published in the Texas Mathematics Teacher (2006) *Teacher Input Into Classroom Visits: Customized Classroom Visit Form.* Ted was also a contributing author for publications from the Charles A. Dana Center: *Mathematics Standards in the Classroom: Resources for Grades 6–8* (2002) and *Middle School Mathematics Assessments: Proportional Reasoning* (2004). He is an active member of Texas Association of Supervisors of Mathematics (TASM) and served on the NCSM Board of Directors as Regional Director for Southern 2. Ted lives with his wife, Susan, in Pflugerville, Texas.

Ruth Harbin Miles coaches rural, suburban, and inner-city school mathematics teachers. Her professional experience includes coordinating the K–12 Mathematics Teaching and Learning Program for the Olathe, Kansas Public Schools for over 25 years; teaching mathematics methods courses at Virginia's Mary Baldwin College and Ottawa University, Mid America Nazarene University, St. Mary's University, and Fort Hays State University in Kansas; and serving as president of the Kansas Association of Teachers of Mathematics. She represented eight Midwestern states on the Board of Directors for the National Council of Supervisors of Mathematics (NCSM) and has been a copresenter for NCSM's Leadership Professional Development National Conferences. Ruth is the coauthor of *Walkway to the Future: How to Implement the NCTM Standards,* (Jansen Publications, 1996), and is one of the writers for NCSM's *PRIME Leadership Framework* (Solution Tree Publishers, 2008). As co-owner of Happy Mountain Learning, she specializes in developing teachers' content knowledge and strategies for engaging students to achieve high standards in mathematics. Ruth resides with her husband Samuel near the Blue Ridge Mountains in Madison, Virginia.

Part I

Preparing the Foundation

1 Understanding and Clarifying Leadership in Mathematics

Today, equity is a top priority for leaders. Indeed, it is listed first in both *the Principles of the National Council of Teachers of Mathematics* (NCTM) and the *PRIME Leadership Framework* of the National Council of Supervisors of Mathematics (NCSM). This prominent location is no accident. Equity is vitally important for leaders in mathematics education, and so it deserves special attention.

Principles and Standards for School Mathematics includes this statement: "Equity requires high expectations and worthwhile opportunities for all" (NCTM, 2000, p. 12). Equity in mathematics achievement, and in all related areas, is critical to the well-being of our nation. To emphasize this need, during 2007 both the NCTM and the NCSM included equity as a strategic priority or as part of a vision statement. Still, the myriad of definitions of equity from various education-related organizations can leave a reader wondering what *equity* really means within education contexts. NCTM has led the way in attempting to answer the question. In 2008, NCTM issued a position statement titled *Equity in Mathematics Education*, which reads in part as follows:

> Excellence in mathematics education rests on equity—high expectations, respect, understanding, and strong support for all students. Policies, practices, attitudes, and beliefs related to mathematics teaching and learning must be assessed continually to ensure that

all students have equal access to the resources with the greatest potential to promote learning. A culture of equity maximizes the learning potential of all students.

The statement notes that joint efforts by educators, students, families, and policymakers are necessary to develop a culture of equity. Such a culture includes, for example, the following characteristics:

- Respecting and valuing each member's contribution
- Acknowledging and embracing experiences, beliefs, and ways of knowing mathematics
- Allocating necessary resources for optimal learning and personal growth
- Expanding the potential for learning through high expectations and culturally relevant practices
- Engaging all students in challenging, rigorous, and meaningful mathematical experiences (NCTM, 2009)

Equity has many important facets, as noted in the above definition, but we have chosen in this book to focus specifically on mathematics leaders' actions that most directly affect student learning and have the greatest chance of closing the achievement gap. This focus is supported by NCSM and detailed in *PRIME Leadership Framework: Principles and Indicators for Mathematics Leaders* (NCSM, 2008). This document stresses that every teacher is responsible for addressing the achievement gap, providing students with meaningful mathematics experiences, and working to erase inequities in student learning.

Every education community has many stakeholders: teachers, students, administrators, parents, and policymakers. Equity is an integral element across the spectrum of the community. Our focus is on the first three stakeholders—teachers, students, and administrators. This focus is not intended to diminish the importance of other stakeholders but to concentrate intentionally on the primary duties and responsibilities of mathematics leaders.

For mathematics leaders, closing the achievement gap must become the highest priority. For decades, the core of our school system has remained fundamentally unchanged. In spite of increased knowledge of inclusive instruction techniques and examples of success, dominant instructional strategies in U.S. schools have remained largely unaltered, thus perpetuating, rather than narrowing, the achievement gap in student performance. In particular, students living in poverty and students of color find it difficult, if not impossible, to succeed in our status quo, noninclusive education system (Achieve, 2006).

Students who do not succeed in mathematics often find that their career opportunities are limited. Advancement, promotion, and pay increases are all linked to one's education (National Mathematics Advisory Panel, 2008). Breaking the cycle of failure in mathematics requires leadership that actively encourages low-income students and students of color to tackle higher-level courses in mathematics—and gives them the tools to succeed with challenging curricula. Such leadership must actively promote a school culture of success, respect, and inclusiveness, along with a healthy appreciation for diversity.

Despite convincing evidence that all students *can* be successful, blaming students for failing rather than seeking ways to help them succeed has been an easy "out" for too many in our education system. Attempts to channel struggling students into so-called remedial programs, though well intentioned, have produced only dismal results. We must— because the future of our nation depends on it—redouble our efforts and reverse the trend of undereducating large numbers of students. A report from the National Research Council (1999) put it this way:

> Many students perform at high levels, but the nation's continued vitality as a democracy and its productivity in a global economy will hinge in the coming decades on the knowledge and skills of the majority—the tens of millions of children who are not realizing their full capacities and are therefore unable to meet the intellectual demands of modern life and work. (p. 7)

Equity can be achieved only if leaders actually lead a process of change. Several developmental stages should help leaders stay focused on equity, including clarifying and articulating the mathematics curriculum, monitoring implementation and curricular rigor, ensuring that every student is learning necessary mathematics, bringing people together into collaborative teams, and redefining professional development. These are among the ideas we will explore throughout this book.

WHAT IS LEADERSHIP AND WHO IS A LEADER?

Readers undoubtedly will realize that definitions of leadership abound. More than 50 can be found simply by doing a quick Internet search, and many are vague or contradictory. For us, writing about leadership, it is important to convey our guiding sense that it is not about a person or a group of people. Rather, leadership is a process.

For the process to be effective, those who direct or facilitate it—the leaders—must act in ways that engender a positive dynamic between them and those with whom they work. Following are two working definitions that we intend to flesh out over the course of this book:

- *Leadership* is the process of influencing work toward a common goal.
- A *leader* is a person who influences individuals or a group to do such work.

These are generic definitions, but they set a foundation. A common goal for mathematics education, and the job most mathematics leaders are hired to do, is to increase student achievement. Implicitly, the goal includes achieving equity by closing the achievement gap. For a leader in mathematics education, reaching this goal requires accomplishing many subgoals. Consequently, leadership must be viewed as a continuous process by which the achievement of one goal leads to taking on a new goal. Leaders are therefore required to be motivators to keep the process going. Leaders empower followers, making them a part of this dynamic process. Each chapter in this book describes a developmental stage or, in some sense, a subgoal of the leadership process.

Throughout this book, we also distinguish between a manager and a leader, in particular an instructional leader. Many people become managers in a variety of educational settings. Their role often is not focused on improving student learning but, in simple terms, on documenting compliance with rules and procedures. This function is necessary, but it is not the focus of this book. *Management* and *leadership* are not interchangeable. Management is a process that keeps organizations, school districts, and schools running smoothly, that keeps things in order and deals with problems that arise within the system. In other words, management maintains the status quo. It does not act as a change agent.

We will assume that successful leaders also practice effective management, as it would be a mistake to disregard this important function. However, we make the distinction between manager and leader to assist educators in seeking and maintaining balance. If only management tasks are completed, needed change does not occur. On the other hand, if excessive change—leaders continually shifting directions—is attempted, then success still will remain elusive. Every mathematics educator has responsibilities in management *and* leadership. To ignore this very important fact would be harmful to the teaching and learning process.

BUILDING A CULTURE OF SUCCESS

Mathematics leaders must guarantee that staff and students are highly valued as individuals and that a culture of success is fostered throughout leaders' areas of influence in a school or district. A culture of success requires an atmosphere of progress and growth. Students and staff members should sense that they are appreciated and valued as vital members of a learning team. Mathematics leaders should be encouragers and supporters, able to answer the following questions in the affirmative:

- Do students and staff members trust each other?
- Does the school promote social equality?
- Is the atmosphere informative and comfortable?
- Are staff members and students treated equitably?
- Is the school climate positive, and are students and teachers recognized for their contributions?

Effective, lasting academic and social changes are built on caring relationships and supportive school environments. In directing the ongoing activities of a school or district, mathematics leaders should maintain this focus. They will find that by supporting positive, cooperative participation in working toward agreed-on goals, one developmental stage at a time, success can be achieved.

Mathematics leaders must be visionaries. They must constantly ponder and facilitate change. However, leaders also need to self-evaluate. Where are they in their own professional development? Where is their district, school, or mathematics department in the broad professional development landscape? Does the curriculum need to be updated to align with state standards? Successfully answering these questions can help lead to the desired culture of success.

NCTM PRINCIPLES AND NCSM LEADERSHIP PRINCIPLES

Mathematics leaders will quickly realize that the principles articulated by the NCTM and the NCSM are highly interrelated. In the chapters that follow, we have not attempted a one-to-one correspondence with either set of principles. Rather, we have tried generally to interweave the principles from NCTM and NCSM throughout the developmental stages.

A brief overview of the two sets of principles, however, may be helpful to lay some groundwork for the material that follows. NCTM's *Principles and Standards for School Mathematics* (2000) sets forth a vision that includes the following:

- Access to high-quality, engaging mathematics instruction
- Ambitious expectations for all

- Knowledgeable teachers with adequate resources and professional development
- Rich mathematics curricula
- Technology as an essential component

NCSM's *PRIME Leadership Framework* (2008) presents a vision focused on leaders and their role in meeting the vision of the NCTM *Principles:*

- Leading the pursuit of a better mathematics future for every child
- Assuming and exercising professional responsibility and accountability for their own practice
- Assuming and exercising professional responsibility and accountability of the teachers they lead

NCTM addresses matters of mathematics curricula in the *Principles* and a companion document, *NCTM Curriculum Focal Points* (2006). These matters include attention to equity, teaching, learning, assessment, and technology. Following are ways in which these topics are viewed:

Equity: High expectations and strong support for all students

Curriculum: Coherent, focused, and well-articulated curriculum

Teaching: Understanding, challenging, and supporting student learning

Learning: Student learning with understanding, actively building new knowledge

Assessment: Useful information to both teachers and students from assessment data

Technology: Use of technology that enhances student learning

The *PRIME* leadership framework from NCSM includes similar emphases:

- Ensure high expectations and access to meaningful mathematics learning for every student.
- Ensure high expectations and access to meaningful mathematics instruction every day.
- Ensure relevant and meaningful mathematics in every lesson.
- Ensure timely, accurate monitoring of student learning and adjustment of teaching instruction for improved student learning.

The following paragraphs illustrate the relationship between the NCTM *Principles* and included factors, and the NCSM *Leadership Indicators.*

To begin, the NCTM *Principles* advocate *high expectations* and *strong support* for all students. These correspond with the NCSM Equity Leadership Indicators:

Equity Leadership Indicator 1: Every teacher addresses gaps in mathematics achievement expectations for all student populations.

Equity Leadership Indicator 2: Every teacher provides each student access to relevant and meaningful mathematics experiences.

Equity Leadership Indicator 3: Every teacher works interdependently in a collaborative learning community to erase inequities in student learning. (p. 9)

In terms of curriculum, three factors from the NCTM *Principles* stand out—coherence, focus, and articulation. These factors correspond with the NCSM Curriculum Leadership Indicators:

Curriculum Leadership Indicator 1: Every teacher implements the local curriculum and uses instructional resources that are coherent and reflect state standards and national curriculum recommendations.

Curriculum Leadership Indicator 2: Every teacher implements a curriculum that is focused on relevant and meaningful mathematics.

Curriculum Leadership Indicator 3: Every teacher implements the intended curriculum with needed intervention and makes certain it is attained by every student. (p. 59)

NCTM separates the Teaching Principle and the Learning Principle, whereas NCSM has combined them. The correspondence between four key factors noted in the NCTM Teaching Principle and the NCSM Teaching and Learning Leadership Indicators is shown below:

1. Effective mathematics teaching requires *understanding what students know*.

   Teaching and Learning Leadership Indicator 3: Every teacher participates in continuous and meaningful mathematics professional development and learning in order to improve his or her practice. (p. 21)

2. Effective mathematics teaching requires *understanding what students need to learn*.

Teaching and Learning Leadership Indicator 1: Every teacher pursues the successful learning of mathematics for every student. (p. 21)

3. Effective mathematics teaching requires *challenging* students to learn mathematics well.

   Teaching and Learning Leadership Indicator 2: Every teacher implements research-informed best practices and uses effective instructional planning and teaching strategies. (p. 21)

4. Effective mathematics teaching requires *supporting* students to learn mathematics well.

   Teaching and Learning Leadership Indicator 1: Every teacher pursues the successful learning of mathematics for every student. (p. 21)

The correspondence between two factors found in the NCTM Learning Principle and the NCSM Teaching and Learning Leadership Indicators is as follows:

1. Students must learn mathematics with understanding.

   Teaching and Learning Leadership Indicator 2: Every teacher implements research-informed best practices and uses effective instructional planning and teaching strategies. (p. 21)

2. Students must *actively build* new knowledge from experience and prior knowledge.

   Teaching and Learning Leadership Indicator 2: Every teacher implements research-informed best practices and uses effective instructional planning and teaching strategies. (p. 21)

The NCTM Assessment Principle provides three key factors. The correspondence between these factors and NCSM Assessment Leadership Indicators is shown below:

1. Assessment should *support* the learning of important mathematics.

   Assessment Leadership Indicator 1: Every teacher uses student assessments that are congruent and aligned by grade level or course content. (p. 45)

2. Assessment should furnish useful information to teachers.

Assessment Leadership Indicator 2: Every teacher uses formative assessment processes to inform teacher practice and student learning. (p. 45)

Assessment Leadership Indicator 3: Every teacher uses summative assessment data to evaluate mathematics grade-level, course, and program effectiveness. (p. 45)

3. Assessment should furnish useful information to students.

Assessment Leadership Indicator 2: Every teacher uses formative assessment processes to inform teacher practice and student learning. (p. 45)

For a visual comparison of the leadership model of this book and the NCTM and NCSM indicators, see Figures 1.1 and 1.2.

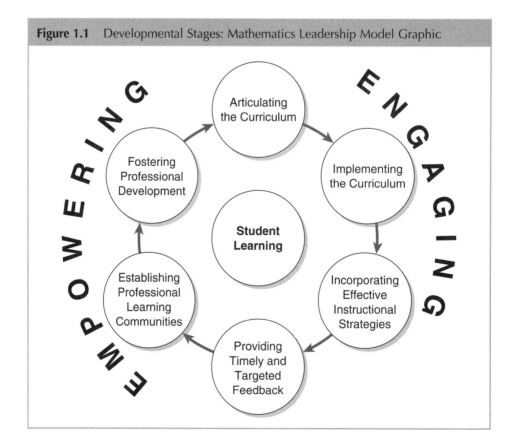

Figure 1.1 Developmental Stages: Mathematics Leadership Model Graphic

Figure 1.2 Aligning the Stages With the Principles

Stages	NCTM/NCSM Principles
● Articulating the Curriculum	Curriculum Principle Curriculum Leadership Principle
● Implementing the Curriculum	Teaching Principle Teaching and Learning Leadership Principle
● Incorporating Effective Instructional Strategies	Learning Principle Teaching and Learning Leadership Principle
● Providing Timely and Targeted Feedback	Assessment Principle Assessment Leadership Principle
● Establishing PLCs and Fostering Professional Development	Pull together elements of each Principle and Leadership Principle for curriculum, teaching, learning, and assessment

The Equity Principle and the Equity Leadership Principle are addressed throughout the stages.

In summary, the first principle and a primary goal is equity, which is approached by ensuring a strong, well-aligned, and successfully implemented mathematics curriculum that provides students opportunities to learn rich, relevant, meaningful mathematics. Implementation of such a curriculum with fidelity requires engaged and empowered teachers who clearly understand mathematics content and possess a wide variety of instructional techniques with which to engage and motivate students.

These same teachers and leaders use data to inform practices—data that help teachers and leaders recognize individual strengths and areas that need attention as well as program strengths and weaknesses. Data analysis and lesson preparation take place in communities of learners who can share ideas and knowledge in a reflective process.

While NCTM and NCSM provide excellent insight into what should be achieved in effective mathematics programs and the goals and actions needed, they do not provide a process for leaders to follow in reaching these goals and performing these actions. This book provides leaders with a plan of action that is reasonable, logical, research based, sequential, and developmental.

2 Engaging and Empowering Staff

Engaging and empowering staff are not developmental stages. These processes cut across the NCTM and NCSM principles of equity, curriculum, teaching, learning, and assessment. However, when fully operational the knowledge and skills embedded in this twin concept of engagement and empowerment are likely to affect equity significantly. Empowered and engaged teachers effectively reach and teach all students the appropriate curriculum. In most cases mathematics leaders will not begin their work with these processes in place. Engagement and empowerment emerge as the developmental stages are implemented.

This chapter is critical for mathematics leaders to read and understand before undertaking developmental processes and procedures to improve student achievement. If leaders do not foster mathematics teachers' participation in improvement processes, then improvement will not go beyond a superficial, show-and-tell level. Without teachers' participation, the best plans and intentions of leaders never get off the ground. Sadly, this frequently has been the case. If mathematics leaders do not understand forces that can, and often do, derail change efforts, then they will be forced to repeat past mistakes, follow familiar trails to dead ends, and fail to institute positive change. This outcome perpetuates the achievement gap.

Efficacy—the personal belief that one can have a positive effect—is a desired outcome of engaging and empowering teachers. Self-efficacy is a necessary component of any change effort (Conzemius & O'Neill, 2001). Teachers need to feel they are part of the system and have a voice in the decisions that directly affect their ability to teach (Covey, 1991). Teachers also must believe that what they do as teachers makes a difference in student learning (Huitt, 2000). Engaging and empowering are not something mathematics leaders do *to* the mathematics staff. Rather, they are the result of actions done *with* the mathematics staff.

This chapter sets a foundation for the leadership actions in the developmental stages described in Chapters 3 through 8. This foundation for working with teachers proceeds from two questions:

1. What are leaders expected to do?

2. What resources can leaders use?

The answers to these questions will help mathematics leaders set in place structures to ensure that teachers are engaged and empowered to achieve successful change.

STAFF INCLUSION AND EFFECTIVE COMMUNICATION

As mathematics leaders undertake efforts to improve teaching and learning, they must maintain a focus on engaging staff in the appropriate actions and empowering staff to take ownership of change efforts. For this to happen, leaders need to include staff in the process and ensure adequate communication. Without structures in place to include staff and to communicate effectively, engagement and empowerment cannot occur.

Including Staff

A high degree of meaningful staff participation is essential. Teachers need to be involved in making decisions that affect instruction. Such involvement empowers teachers. Therefore, it is essential for mathematics leaders to provide opportunities by which teachers can support one another and collaborate to achieve change. Empowerment involves increasing teachers' perception of their personal power to improve teaching and learning. Short and Greer (2002) comment,

> Power is thought to be an infinite commodity that is available to accomplish the goals and mission of the organization. To expand the amount of power, one involves additional persons in the decisions of the organization. The saying, "the principal gains power by giving it away" appears to sum up the process. (p. 14)

By this notion mathematics leaders increase teachers' personal power perception by increasing teachers' inclusion in decision making about curriculum and instruction.

One of the best research-documented structures for encouraging participation in the decision-making process and sharing power for students' learning is collaborative teaming (Kanold, 2005; Dukewits & Gowin, 1996). Leaders should understand that team efforts are based on the emergence of teacher leadership. Although there should be flexibility within a team, teachers should be encouraged to accept leadership roles based on interest, ability, experience, and initiative. Developing and operating collaborative teams requires the intertwining of various leadership functions. Teacher team leaders act as extensions of the authority of principals. Teacher leaders need the power to schedule, plan, attend, and guide regular team meetings. They are charged with responsibilities to maintain the focus of such meetings on student achievement, instructional strategies, content, pacing, success, and intervention.

Communicating Effectively

In addition to including staff, leaders must set in place structures for encouraging open, honest communication. Part of a process for empowering teachers means opening the classroom door in order to make teachers' educational practices overt and thus improve communication. Classroom visits to support the implementation of instructional strategies are one means of accomplishing this. By entering classrooms to provide support, leaders gain credibility for their observations and recommendations. In Chapter 4 we discuss in greater depth strategies and approaches recommended to enter classrooms and effectively gather and share supportive data.

Teachers also should be encouraged to visit their colleagues' classrooms to stay informed and to develop a sense of community. According to Williams (1996), "Peer pressure, when coupled with valued professional feedback, increases teacher engagement. Teachers do their best work when they collaborate with demanding colleagues" (p. 135). Peer pressure, frequently referred to as a negative influence, can exert a positive influence when team members recognize that they are invaluable to the success of the team. This sense of belonging to a community and recognizing the vital role each member plays encourages individuals to succeed. Pressure to cooperate rather than pressure to compete is supported when classrooms are open and visible.

Another aspect of communication involves charting the progress of students affected by the collaborative team's decisions. Leaders need to gather student achievement data and communicate them to team members and principals. This also is essential in order to build trust. By ensuring that collaborative, collegial efforts are directed toward improving student achievement and by sharing the results of collaboration through open communication, leaders share power and thus build trust. Trust, in turn, is essential to maintaining and strengthening shared power.

As leaders move into and through the developmental stages in a mathematics leadership model, they will be required to examine the ways they include teachers in change processes and the ways they create and maintain open lines of communication. Including staff in decision making and ensuring effective communication are critical factors for implementing change. These two factors provide the groundwork for engaging and empowering staff, but they are not sufficient by themselves to accomplish success.

LEADERSHIP DECISION MAKING

Leaders are bombarded with questions and continually sought out to solve problems both major and minor. Before leaders can decide what to do about the major ones, they must consider several questions, such as the following:

- What are we trying to improve?
- What has been done already?
- What is the current status of the issue or problem?
- What would an effective solution look like?
- Who is involved?
- What resources are needed?
- What amount of time is the issue or problem likely to take?
- What is the priority (do other improvements hinge on this one)?

Only critical issues or problems merit this amount of effort. But then, what are critical issues or problems and what are not? What will be the effect of this decision on other issues? What decisions should mathematics leaders make, what decisions should teachers make, and what decisions should reside with other leaders?

There is insufficient time for one person to solve all the issues, even the important ones. There is only sufficient time and energy when issues are addressed by groups of people. And that will happen only if mathematics leaders can foster commitment or ownership among the individuals in those groups.

INSTRUCTIONAL LEADERSHIP

Leaders intuitively know to communicate with staff and to involve staff in decision making if they expect improvement initiatives to succeed. Why then has there been such limited success at closing the achievement gap in student performance and increasing student success generally in mathematics? Part of the answer resides with the current way that many decisions are made. Superficial, misdirected efforts at involvement with insufficient knowledge of the change process do not work. Leaders must achieve a new depth of understanding about engaging and empowering staff, targeted at changing actions and eventually beliefs.

As mathematics teachers become more deeply involved in decision making and become engaged in teaching an aligned curriculum, they will begin to see a dramatic change in their students' mathematics learning. When teachers are engaged in effective practices, students are more responsive. Teachers who deepen their awareness of the direct effect they have on student learning will engage in teaching an appropriate curriculum. All of this will begin a positive upward spiral of achievement and should affirm belief in teaching to high expectations. But maintaining momentum and steering the proper course of action also demand continuing leadership.

Specifically, *instructional* leadership needs to emerge to change classroom practices in mathematics. Instructional leadership is an element within the broad spectrum of leadership skills targeted at improving student achievement. A dire need for new instructional leadership has arisen from the repeated failure of public schools to close the achievement gap in student performance, as well as from a general erosion of public confidence in schools (Short & Greer, 2002). For substantive change to occur, mathematics leaders need to analyze the current instructional model and formulate a new vision.

Current Beliefs and Behaviors—and Resistance

During previous decades numerous school initiatives were launched to improve student achievement in mathematics. However, after an initial flurry of activity and perhaps even a modicum of success, these efforts faded and results diminished. With the advent of No Child Left Behind legislation, schools once again feel pressure to produce results, yet success has still remained elusive.

Marzano (2003) states that the classroom teacher is the single most important factor in student learning. If this is true, and we believe it is, then it is important to understand why change initiatives have failed repeatedly to substantively alter teachers' beliefs about classroom instruction and their instructional behaviors. Effecting change means that we need to study the current system, or structure, that sustains and reinforces beliefs and practices that are ineffective.

When change efforts are set in motion in schools, other forces immediately align to counteract them. Some resistance is intentional, but some is simply inherent in the system (or any system). After all, change can be uncomfortable. It usually requires altering patterns of behavior that have grown comfortable, even if they are less than optimally successful. And change takes energy. Leaders who want to propel sustainable change must understand these natural tendencies toward systemic inertia. If they do not, then any change initiative will probably grind to a halt sooner or later.

The nature of a system is to strive for equilibrium, a balance among beliefs and behaviors that will tend to maintain the status quo. Stability certainly is not a bad thing; people need predictability. However, equilibrium forces also work against change—unless new energy is found to push the system out of balance and force those in the system to adopt new beliefs and behaviors. Change is sustained when systems achieve and then can maintain a new equilibrium. As Kaser and colleagues (2001) point out: "Successful change initiatives evolve over time from initiation to implementation and, finally, to institutionalization" (p. 62).

Unfortunately, school systems, it seems, rarely get past initiation. Change initiatives may knock them off balance briefly, but the old equilibrium returns, inertia reasserts itself, and they are back to the status quo.

Thompson (2003) provides a glimpse of the status quo found in many school systems. In his article "Creating a High-Performance School System" he states the issue well:

> For all of the fluidity and dynamism of school districts as social systems, the fundamental features of their underlying culture and structure tend to be stubbornly inert. It's a well-known fact that the

modern public school and the school district are direct descendants of the Industrial Revolution. Public schools were modeled after factories, and factories were built to last. Factories have traditionally been designed with an eye toward optimizing efficiency through regimented processes. A blood relative of such regimentation is aversion to change. (p. 489)

If change is to occur, educators must continue reform efforts with a goal of breaking the grip of the factory model (Short & Greer, 2002).

In mathematics, a systemic status quo works hand in hand with a classroom status quo. The two have reached equilibrium; they are well balanced. For the most part, the school system supports and maintains the operation of the classroom. A hallmark for capturing the current state of the mathematics classroom is the Third International Mathematics and Science Study (TIMSS; now named Trends in International Mathematics and Science Study) report. According to the *National Commission on Mathematics and Science Teaching for the 21st Century* (2000) the TIMSS report typifies instruction in mathematics and science classrooms as lecture and skill practice. The subject area is covered, and the primary resource is the adopted textbook. Student engagement in the learning process is minimal and usually optional. There is a consistent pattern of classroom teaching, which consists of

1. a review of previous material and homework;

2. a problem illustration by the teacher;

3. drills on low-level procedures that imitate those demonstrated by the teacher;

4. supervised seatwork by students, often in isolation;

5. checking of seatwork problems; and

6. assignment of homework. (p. 20)

Even though TIMMS shows that this current instructional structure is not effective for many students, significant change in instructional strategies has not occurred to any significant degree. Lack of student success alone is not enough to motivate systemic or classroom-based change. Evidence supports the idea of fundamentally resistant systemwide structures, which support current instructional behaviors and maintain the status quo. To change this system, instructional leadership specific to mathematics teaching and learning is needed.

Leveraging Staff

Appropriating a banking term, we use *leverage* in its verb form, meaning "to use borrowed capital for an investment." (McKean, 2005). *Leveraging staff* refers to drawing capital—energy, ideas, and so on—from staff that can be invested in the change initiative in order to generate success.

Change requires energy. While the demand for change may be present, finding a source of energy for change can be more challenging. Substantive change takes initial energy—energy to scale up—and sustaining energy to maintain the change initiative until the system has gained a new equilibrium. Leaders alone cannot provide all of the needed energy (Reeves, 2006).

An obvious source of additional energy is classroom teachers. The *National Commission on Mathematics and Science Teaching for the 21st Century* (2000) states that "after an extensive, in-depth review of what is happening in our classrooms, the Commission has concluded that the most powerful instrument for change, and therefore the place to begin, lies at the very core of education—with teaching itself" (p. 5). Teacher efficacy is the most available resource for increasing student learning. Teachers must be leveraged to initiate and sustain change.

Efficacy appears to have two major components. Williams, in her book, *Closing the Achievement Gap* (1996), refers to these two components when she states that "unless teachers *engage* in teaching and feel that they are *effective*, students are less likely to make rapid progress in learning" (p. 8, emphasis added). Empowerment conveys the belief that one's actions are effective. For purposes of this book, we equate effectiveness with empowerment and use engagement and empowerment as means of leveraging staff to supply energy for change.

DYNAMICS OF ENGAGEMENT AND EMPOWERMENT

Mathematics leaders who intend to tap the energy of teachers and institute change initiatives must understand the dynamics of engagement and empowerment. Engagement and empowerment reside on a continuum ranging from resistance and lack of change to improvement and sustained change. Lack of engagement or empowerment is negative in that its absence absorbs or diffuses energy that is needed to initiate and sustain change.

Another way to look at the dynamics of engagement and empowerment is to set these concepts on an axis, as shown in Figure 2.1. The four quadrants represent the presence or absence of engagement and empowerment. For example, the first quadrant (Q1) is the presence of both engagement and empowerment, two positives (+, +). The third quadrant (Q3) illustrates the opposite, the absence of both engagement and empowerment, thus two negatives (–, –). The plus and minus symbols indicate whether energy is added or subtracted when leaders and staff operate within the given quadrant. Optimally, mathematics leaders want to leverage staff in order to operate consistently in Q1.

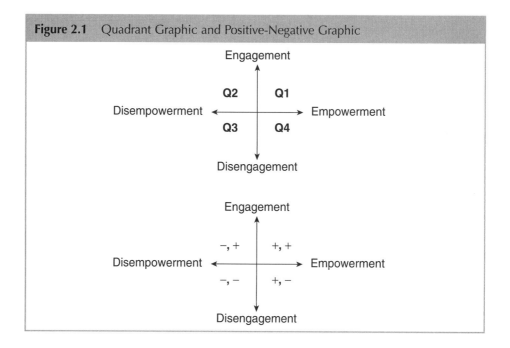

Figure 2.1   Quadrant Graphic and Positive-Negative Graphic

Education research has not sufficiently analyzed or appreciated the interactions between these forces, even though disengagement and disempowerment are addressed in education literature. School leaders who fail to consider all aspects of these forces and inadvertently or by design consign professionals to work in disengaged, isolated settings, with the likely result of disempowerment, will fail to generate the energy necessary to initiate effective instructional change.

These ideas were expressed more than twenty years ago. For example, Tye and Tye (1984) suggested that "we failed with the earlier reforms, and we will fail with the current reforms, because we refuse to face the realities of what it takes to change such complex social/political institutions as schools" (p. 319). Their observation was predictive and has proven true again and again. Too often leaders have asked disengaged and disempowered teachers to provide the energy for sustainable change, thereby dooming the change initiative before it was ever launched.

However, repeated failure to create lasting change in the past should not be an excuse to stop trying. Instead, mathematics leaders need to understand the forces of resistance and plan to address them when instituting efforts to change instructional methods and increase the chances for all students to succeed. Educators have learned how to counteract the resistance forces in schools by using collaborative strategies that engage and empower teachers who deal directly with student learning (Short & Greer, 2002).

A closer look at disengagement, engagement, disempowerment, and empowerment may prove helpful as a way to conclude this chapter and set the stage for the chapters that follow.

Disengagement (–) is nothing new. Part of disengagement is systemic: teachers commonly work in relatively isolated situations (Short & Greer, 2002). Isolation is a persistent problem in education and contributes to disengagement, but disengagement goes deeper than merely working in isolation. Disengaged teachers often are given freedom to teach content they elect to teach in a style of their choosing, regardless of school or district plans or initiatives. While there may be a required curriculum, there is no concomitant requirement for teachers to teach it. Disengagement is a result of low expectations and little or no accountability. While this probably is not the intent of school leaders—or teachers—it is one reality.

Teachers working in isolated situations have little opportunity to share ideas or reflect on teaching and learning with colleagues. Teachers may believe that all mathematics teachers in a school behave similarly. But in actuality five teachers could have five different sets of instructional beliefs and teaching strategies and never realize it (Reeves, 2006). This echoes Short and Greer (2002): "Teachers are isolated in most school settings, and their work is rarely collegial in most typical schools (Little, 1982). This professional isolation is the greatest impediment to learning to teach" (p. 145). Indeed, in isolation many teachers may not even try proposed new strategies.

To counteract the effects of disengagement, mathematics leaders must first encourage classroom teachers to be engaged. Engagement (+) is involvement in the activities of a school or district and has two dimensions. The first dimension is personal engagement in the adopted curriculum. The second is collaborative engagement, working collegially as members of a team. These dimensions of engagement are critical to alignment and coherence in curriculum, referred to by Fenwick English (2000) as the "written, taught, and tested" curriculum and by Robert Marzano (2003) as the "guaranteed and viable" curriculum. The foundation for students' opportunity to learn appropriate content is formed here. And most teachers truly want to be involved in decisions about curriculum implementation that directly affect their teaching (Short & Greer, 2002).

Addressing the engagement/disengagement continuum alone will not ensure effective change. The empowerment/disempowerment continuum also must be addressed. This continuum is related to beliefs, and the dynamics are therefore harder to recognize. In an article on teacher efficacy Huitt (2000) quotes from Ashton's 1984 research that emphasized the importance of teacher beliefs. Ashton identified a need for teachers, first, to believe that students are able to learn the content. Coupled with this is a second belief that students are able to learn the content from their instruction. Energy to sustain change does not come from teachers who believe they are unempowered, or do not have the power to influence student learning.

Empowerment (+) is a belief that one's energy, effort, or behavior will result in specific positive outcomes that are reliable and recognized. For mathematics teachers this means that they are aware that what they do matters with regard to student learning (Short & Greer, 2002). The sense of empowerment emerges over time as individuals, working in a supportive, collaborative mathematics team, see evidence of success.

Disempowerment (–) is a belief that student success or failure comes about because of factors, conditions, or problems that are outside the control of the school or the teacher. Responsibility is displaced. Disempowerment amounts to learned helplessness. Statements that indicate a sense of disempowerment may include references to a student's home life, innate abilities (or their absence), or motivation. These are reality buffers that can prevent change initiatives from taking root and thriving. After all, if you do not see that your actions make a difference, why change? This inability to make a difference may lead to burnout—the withdrawal of energy and loss of commitment. In all probability, burnout arises from this continuous inability to make a difference rather than an overcommitment to a heavy work schedule (Fullan, 1993). It is debilitating to face failure on a regular basis. Surviving in an isolated environment may well mean blaming failure on factors outside one's control, which can erode teachers' confidence in their ability to teach and thus alter teachers' expectations of students' ability to learn.

Engagement and empowerment go hand in hand. Teachers who teach an adopted, aligned mathematics curriculum and use recommended strategies gain ownership of student achievement. They see the results of their efforts. Likewise, disengagement and disempowerment go hand-in-hand. Teachers who routinely deviate from adopted course content and use only a limited range of instructional techniques do not see optimal results from their efforts, nor do they accept ownership of them.

To better understand the dynamics of engagement and empowerment, characteristics that would typify teachers in each quadrant contained in Figure 2.1 are offered in Figure 2.2, Empowerment-Engagement Continuum.

Figure 2.2 Empowerment-Engagement Continuum

Quadrant II (Disempowered, Engaged) (−,+)	Quadrant I (Empowered, Engaged) (+,+)
Teachers enjoy social functions and meetings. They are easy to work with and serve on multiple committees. They may well believe that school should be a "fun" place and are willing to go the "extra mile" for students. While agreeable, and making every effort to conform to expectations, these teachers do not believe they have any control over student learning, which is probably viewed as some form of a natural gift. They do the best with what they have. Easier classes are readily recommended, since students are working to their ability and should not be overwhelmed or discouraged. Time in structured meetings is devoted to topics that are less directly related to student learning such as classroom management, parent contacts, grading, or scheduling.	Teachers believe in the power of collaboration for students and teachers. They recognize the responsibility that comes with teaching and challenge every student to succeed. They strive to teach the designated curriculum in more depth and with greater understanding. They expect every student to be successful and work hard to prove it true. They also challenge every mathematics teacher to reach high expectations and then surpass them. Sharing, reflecting, and improving are critical parts of every activity, lesson, and professional development opportunity. The collective energy of the group is greater than the sum of the individual's energy. These are the groups of educators who will "do whatever it takes" to ensure student success. The attitude exemplified by this group of educators (whatever it takes) is strongly correlated to student and school success.
Quadrant III (Disempowered, Disengaged) (−,−)	Quadrant IV (Empowered, Disengaged) (+,−)
Teachers work by themselves with no feelings of responsibility or empowerment and don't feel that what they do actually makes a difference in student learning. They view themselves as dispensers of mathematical content knowledge. Learning particular content is attributed to an innate ability or desire of the student—the "math gene." This does not mean to imply any antisocial behavior. Indeed, teachers may be well liked and respected. The belief, however, is that learning is due to factors outside of the teachers' control, while what and how they teach mathematics is their absolute domain. Disempowered/disengaged teachers may easily select content that is not grade-level appropriate. In most cases, this content is below grade level rather than above it. In either case, students suffer.	Teachers work alone. As with Quadrant III teachers, they feel that what and how they teach is their domain. However, they are very open with what they do. Possibly, they are excellent teachers and serve their particular students well. They believe in themselves and their ability to teach, but probably doubt other teachers can match their ability or even want to try. Teamwork, staff meetings, and inservice days just "aren't their thing."

In his article "Tipping Point," Schmoker (2004) states, "We can no longer afford to be innocent of the fact that 'collaboration' improves performance" (p. 431). Effective collaboration must ensure that groups of teachers and administrators are both engaged and empowered in work that directly and positively affects student learning. If educators at all levels of a school system are not actively engaged and empowered, then the forces of equilibrium will defeat any change initiative and reassert the status quo.

EXPECTATIONS AND CHALLENGES

Engagement and empowerment of mathematics teachers will result in increased student learning and achievement (Conzemius & O'Neill, 2001). Therefore, mathematics leaders will be expected to direct their efforts toward providing the settings, collaboration, and actions necessary for engagement and empowerment to flourish in a school or district.

The actions of effective mathematics leaders must evince empathy, concern, and a driving passion for improving student learning and achievement. Improvement efforts do not effect change overnight, and so the work toward improvement must be sustained over time. Furthermore, all interested parties must be as deeply involved and engaged as their leaders are. Mathematics leaders set academic goals. They sustain focus on achieving desired results. And they work with teachers in establishing a common vision of what an effective mathematics classroom should look like and how adopted mathematics curriculum documents can support this vision.

Maintaining the momentum of reform is key. Teaming, collaboration, trust, and involvement evolve over time. Leaders set the pace and evaluate it against observed changes in instructional behaviors. Leaders must persist, often in spite of setbacks. Teachers and others will exhibit various levels of participation, knowledge, and results. There also will be varying degrees of willingness to participate, and leaders cannot expect staff to remain static—teachers transfer or retire, and new teachers take their place. Thus leaders must be sensitive to the needs of newcomers as well as the needs of those already in the midst of change.

This book is intended for mathematics leaders, but the content should not be a secret from teachers, other subject leaders, administrators, or other staff. The ideas, suggestions, and recommendations we present are transparent and above board. The preceding information about engagement and empowerment, for example, should be discussed and reflected on by all parties. This is part of the teaching-learning equation, which mathematics leaders must exemplify.

Part II

A Leadership Model

3 Articulating the Curriculum

The word *curriculum* has various definitions and is used by educators to refer to many aspects of what teachers teach and students learn. For purposes of this book, *curriculum* is a district-developed document that translates national, state, and local standards into an organized, developmental plan of learning objectives tied to accompanying materials for student use (programs, texts, other resources) and lesson designs for teachers to use. How well a curriculum addresses these components, aligns to the state standards, assists teachers and students in identifying mathematics concepts, and provides well-designed lessons determines the strength of the curriculum.

Marzano (2003) cites the Second International Mathematics Study (SIMS) in identifying three types of curricula: the intended curriculum, the implemented curriculum, and the attained curriculum. These three types are reinforced by research conducted by Fenwick English on the effects of alignment between written, taught, and tested curricula (English, 2000). Each of these three curricula is essential to student learning. If one of the three goes awry, then equity is challenged and the performance gap between student populations widens. This chapter focuses on the intended, or written, curriculum. Chapter 4 focuses on the implemented, or taught, curriculum, and Chapter 6 focuses on the attained, or tested, curriculum.

The interrelationships among these three curricula cannot be over emphasized. We address them in three different chapters, but they work together. Coherence among what is written, what is taught, and what is assessed is the foundation for equitable achievement (English, 2000). Nonetheless, they also should be seen as developmental. The intended curriculum is the foundation for the implemented one, and the implemented curriculum provides the foundation for the attained one.

CURRICULUM ALIGNMENT

Teachers and students should not be held accountable for course or grade-level content that is not clearly articulated or defined. Holding teachers and students accountable on state or district assessments that do not match intended course content is reprehensible. Instructional leaders are charged with responsibility for ensuring a rigorous and equitable mathematics curriculum that is aligned. The alignment of written, taught, and tested curricula is essential to this task and is a cornerstone for success in student achievement (English, 2000). In his book, *What Works In Schools: Translating Research into Action,* Marzano (2003) insists that education research strongly indicates that an aligned and "viable" (the assurance that the objectives can be taught within the allotted time) curriculum is a major factor in successful schools. Alignment and viability provide a necessary foundation for student access to appropriate mathematics curriculum content.

What Are Leaders Expected to Do?

A basic element of success for mathematics leaders and the students to whom they are responsible is getting every mathematics teacher teaching the intended curriculum every day. The idea is so basic that one would assume that the intended curriculum would be exacting, precise, and detailed. However, nothing could be further from the truth. States, districts, schools, and classrooms offer incredibly broad and diverse mathematics content (National Mathematics Advisory Panel, 2008). A job for mathematics leaders within their sphere of influence and control is to address the idea of an intended curriculum with staff. Teachers need to understand what content is to be taught before they are held accountable for teaching it.

Coherence, or alignment, between intended, implemented, and attained curricula is paramount for student achievement. While school districts often achieve a high degree of coherence for their local curriculum, they sometimes fail to understand that dual systems are operating. Every state, because of No Child Left Behind legislation, has some form of intended curriculum and an assessment to determine student acquisition of content. Mathematics leaders are expected to verify, not assume, that dual systems (local and state) are highly coordinated and aligned. Content intended by a state to be taught at the course or grade level should be the content contained in district curriculum documents.

Mathematics leaders recognize that curriculum alignment is a district-level job and not one to be decided at the school or classroom level. To be effective, a curriculum should be vertically and horizontally seamless across a district for every teacher in every grade and in every course. To ensure that this is the case, mathematics leaders are expected to coordinate and facilitate the work of alignment. Teams of teachers and leaders are expected to engage in the process of understanding the curriculum and building consensus on course and grade-level mathematics content.

Leaders Ensure Curriculum Alignment

To ensure that state content standards are being addressed and that teachers know where standards are embedded in a program, mathematics leaders must arrange to have mathematics teachers, or a subgroup of the staff, carefully study content standards. Engaging in and facilitating frequent, meaningful conversations about curriculum is a job responsibility of leaders.

Unfortunately, these necessary conversations often are avoided or blocked because principals or other administrators find them to be confusing, intimidating, or unworthy of the time to be spent. Mathematics leaders, unless authorized to call meetings independently, must work closely and respectfully with administrators to alleviate this problem. Understanding administrators' job responsibilities and being empathetic to pressures and demands made on administrators are worthy tasks for mathematics leaders.

In working toward curriculum alignment mathematics leaders would do well to attend to three points. First, individual states generally create learner objectives under various mathematics strands, such as numbers and operations, algebra and functions, measurement, geometry, data analysis, and probability. This organizational list works well for identifying content scope, and it aids in vertical alignment of a curriculum. However, it is not an arrangement easily transformed into an instructional guide for classroom teachers. Mathematics leaders who merely hand teachers state standards should recognize that, while this is an important step, it is insufficient to ensure effective instruction. An approach like this tends to foster a "checklist" view of teaching rather than a "conceptual" approach to learning. At the same time, it also should be remembered that a standards document is different from a curriculum document. Teachers may believe that a textbook or a curriculum covers the standards without actually checking to be sure.

Second, in the United States there is one dominant instructional technique employed by classroom mathematics teachers to the virtual exclusion of other, more effective methods (National Commission on Mathematics and Science Teaching for the 21st Century, 2000). It is so prevalent that it can be safely assumed that whatever influence teachers have on student learning, this technique can be directly associated with the results, whether positive or negative. In essence, the traditional instructional pattern of lecture, then demonstration, followed by independent student practice on worksheets has not changed in many, many years. This approach is so entrenched that alternative approaches are routinely screened out. Materials and instructional techniques that differ from this approach are often disregarded without fair analysis. In such an environment the dissemination of standards documents alone will have little effect.

Third, in the report, "A Nation at Risk" (1983), from the National Commission on Education, the U.S. mathematics curriculum was referred to as one that is a mile wide and an inch deep. The fact that content contained in curriculum documents often appears very broad and very shallow means that teachers believe they cannot meet the alignment demand set by English nor the viability standard established by Marzano. This belief frequently is a result of the first factor, in which the curriculum is seen as a teaching checklist of disconnected skills rather than a cluster of concept-related ones. Because of this instructional approach and an "inch-deep" curriculum, mathematics content expands each year to encompass the preceding year's content. A felt need to review the previous year's content for the first six weeks of school virtually ensures that the current year's content will not be adequately covered, much less taught to mastery. This belief is reinforced when mathematics teachers are handed textbooks, curriculum guides, course syllabi, and state standards as disconnected, stand-alone documents.

Leaders in mathematics must conduct regular meetings to address these challenges to the curriculum. They must also diplomatically bring the three influencing factors to administrators for discussion. Without firm leadership these three factors will exert tremendous influence on a mathematics curriculum-development process with the result that, in all likelihood, the status quo will be maintained.

Resources That Leaders Can Use

Leaders and others involved in working on a district curriculum need a thorough knowledge of the National Council of Teachers of Mathematics' *Principals and Standards for School Mathematics* (NCTM, 2000), the related NCTM *Curriculum Focal Points* (2006), their current curriculum documents, state standards, and mathematics content. Based on this information, a staff must locate the standards in the local program, highlight these standards, and match the depth of the program to the depth of the standards. Teachers may choose to teach mathematics at more depth than state standards, but they must not elect to teach it to a lesser depth. By reviewing how standards can be assessed, teachers also will gain a better feel for how lessons should be structured.

Principals and Standards for School Mathematics identifies 10 standards to supply a framework for a well-developed, comprehensive mathematics program. Five of these standards are content: number and operations, algebra, geometry, measurement, and data analysis and probability. The remaining five are process standards: problem solving, reasoning and proof, communication, connections, and representation. Mathematics leaders should use these as a measuring tool to evaluate their curricula. The process standards supply students with access to content, aid retention, and develop conceptual understanding. The process standards are the glue that holds the mathematics content together. They must be an integral part of any comprehensive curriculum (NCTM, 2000).

OPPORTUNITY TO LEARN

Our society is increasingly diverse and mobile, and our economy is international. Students who have managed to pass only watered-down algebra and geometry courses are competing for jobs with students who have successfully completed four or more years of rigorous high school mathematics (National Mathematics Advisory Panel, 2008). According to NCTM (2000), "Well-documented examples demonstrate that all children, including those who have been traditionally underserved, can learn mathematics when they have access to high-quality instructional programs that support their learning" (p. 14). How mathematics leaders address this challenge will have a dramatic effect on our nation and future generations (National Mathematics Advisory Panel, 2008).

Opportunity to learn an appropriate curriculum forms a basis for closing the achievement gap (English, 2000). It has the strongest relationship with student achievement of all the school-level factors identified in a meta-analysis of research on school success (Marzano,

2003). Opportunity to learn appropriate mathematics content relies heavily on teachers teaching the appropriate content. Therefore, articulating the curriculum and ensuring its implementation is vital.

What Are Leaders Expected to Do?

Opportunity to learn has three elements. The first opportunity, discussed in the previous section, is for written course content to match intended course content. Second is that students actually take the intended or desired courses. Third, and most important, students are successful in these courses.

Once a curriculum document matches the desired course content, then the course taught must match the prescribed content. It should not be up to the teacher to choose mathematics content. We know that students who are struggling and those from poverty backgrounds often are assigned to the least experienced teachers (Love, 2004). Less experienced teachers tend to dilute content and thus deny students rigorous content. Consequently, these students fall increasingly further behind their peers. The downward spiral of denied opportunity and access is devastating to students in greatest need. All "schools must provide maximum opportunity-to-learn, by which we mean not merely course titles, but course substance" (Adelman, 2006, p. 108).

Mathematics leaders need to ensure equitable access to courses by carefully monitoring barriers to participation. A rigorous mathematics course aligned to state standards serves no purpose unless students are actually encouraged to take the course. Barriers may reside in a district or school without consciously being seen as preventing students from participating in higher mathematics. For example, a district may use a form of tracking that begins in elementary or middle school and includes "accelerating" identified students. Those not accelerated are, essentially, left behind. Or a school might administer placement tests disguised as diagnostic exams, which slot students into specific courses. These exams function as a barrier for students whose parents do not challenge the results, do not have the resources to retest their child independently, or cannot afford to hire a tutor. Tracking also may occur if teachers select students for their classes or students are required to get permission from teachers or counselors before registering for courses. Another barrier arises when parents are allowed to designate a preferred teacher. Scheduling can put up other barriers: certain courses are offered only at certain times, or enrollment is limited.

Course scheduling conflicts do occur. There also are valid reasons for diagnostic tests and even justifications for placing certain students with certain teachers. Mathematics leaders are expected to ensure that such things are not systematic barriers and do not discriminate against specific populations.

Leaders Ensure Opportunity to Learn

One initiative is that mathematics leaders should work with other instructional leaders and administrators to reduce the number of remedial mathematics courses. In the United States a trend in mathematics has been to create less-demanding courses for students who struggle with the traditional approach to teaching. Failure has been blamed on students' innate lack of mathematics ability. Current research is showing the error of this thinking. Students' degree of effective effort is proving to be the key, not genetics. Through belief in effort, students who have not traditionally achieved in mathematics can successfully learn mathematics. The greatest effect occurs when students are confronted with evidence that their effort is critical to learning, not their "math gene" (National Research Council, 2005). Mathematics leaders need to obtain districtwide agreement—from superintendent to teacher—to reduce remedial courses in a timely manner. Students will never catch up academically in an education system that continually slows them down.

Mathematics leaders need to monitor use of placement tests as screening devices that might exclude students from specific courses. The temptation to believe that certain skills are required for successful completion of a course is strong. In some cases this may be true. However, when skills are applied to solve meaningful, challenging problems, students actually learn the skills better than in a disconnected approach (National Research Council, 2005).

Diagnostic assessments can be effectively used to help students succeed in mathematics courses when such assessments highlight strengths and weaknesses of mathematical understanding. These identified strengths and weaknesses should be used to scaffold skills at an appropriate time during instruction to increase the likelihood of student success. Mathematics leaders may use tests to analyze the effectiveness of certain lessons or units, but the results should not be used as evidence to include or exclude certain students from participating.

Mathematics leaders should carefully review the composition of various mathematics classes to ensure against improper screening out of students. One approach is to monitor passing and participation rates matched to ethnicity and gender. If even one traditionally underserved population is absent in certain courses, such as upper-level courses, the system must be scrutinized to discover a cause. Furthermore, if a disproportionate number of underserved students make up the majority in tracked or remedial courses, leaders must directly confront the problem.

For example, course tracking for algebra may begin in sixth grade or earlier. Mathematics leaders have two fronts on which to address the inequity issue. Tracking can be confronted in the sixth grade, and course participation can be confronted when students take algebra. However, simply fixing the problem in sixth grade and then waiting for those students to reach algebra is not acceptable because such a limited approach closes the door of opportunity for too many students.

Leaders must work with teachers and administrators to provide ongoing intervention and remediation inside and outside of classrooms. The temptation in intervention or remediation is simply to repeat the lesson or to send students to generic tutoring or lab sessions that emphasize skill-building rather than course-specific content understanding. Students need help learning the current material for a course in which they are enrolled. Adding disconnected skill and drill is more likely to interfere with learning than to facilitate it. Classroom lessons must be designed with embedded skills to provide students with the tools they need to overcome skill deficits. Effective remediation efforts directly address content that a student is confronting in the classroom. Most importantly, intervention and remediation programs need to be established that provide students with alternative ways to learn content, not just more problems using the same instructional methods.

To stay informed, mathematics leaders also should regularly talk to students. Why do students think they are successful or unsuccessful? What do they like about a course? What would help them be successful? One of the first factors for a mathematics leader to check is students' behaviors—in this case, not so much whether they are disruptive, but are they unproductive? Schools often have policies that overly penalize students for failure to complete homework. In other cases only one form of assessment is used to determine course success. Perhaps departmental or districtwide tests do not accurately reflect the taught content.

Students may also may need help understanding life choices related to academic course selection. Choosing certain high school courses can radically affect available career possibilities as well as future learning opportunities. A large number of students aspire to continue in some form of higher education after high school. However, the American Diploma Project notes that many are unprepared to do so (Achieve, 2004, 2006). Mathematics leaders should lead this communication effort by regularly gathering and organizing data about mathematics achievement and career choices. They need to work with counselors, students, and parents to disseminate such information throughout middle schools and high schools. Particular attention should be given to providing female students with information about women in mathematics and related fields, as they are an underserved population in many cases when it comes to mathematics.

Particularly in middle and high schools, mathematics leaders need to build strong communication networks with counselors. Understanding course criteria and expectations is imperative for adults who work with students. Counselors can serve as advocates for students. For example, they can work to keep students in more rigorous mathematics courses where the students might receive a C grade, rather than taking the easier path of moving students to less demanding courses. In too many cases after students have completed the required number of mathematics credits, they are counseled out of further mathematics even though they are capable. Parents, teachers, counselors, and the students themselves should be aware of the effects of this choice on college degree completion (Achieve, 2004).

School counselors also are an excellent resource for identifying patterns of student access and success. In working with student schedules and grades, counselors frequently detect issues or concerns. Even though they may not have "hard data" to back up their suspicions, mathematics leaders can use this intuition to verify or refute their suspicions. Close working relationships with counselors help alert mathematics leaders to emerging issues that can be addressed before they become significant problems.

Resources That Leaders Can Use

Mathematics leaders might begin with state information on course content. Anything related to course content sanctioned by a state should be collected and carefully reviewed. Leaders also must become well informed about pertinent information from professional organizations, such as the National Council of Teachers of Mathematics. Leaders may use reference information from national assessments, such as the National Assessment of Educational Progress (NAEP).

Career information and recommendations about preparing for the world of work found in business or government publications also can help mathematics leaders provide current information about careers involving mathematics to teachers, counselors, administrators, and others.

SCOPE, SEQUENCE, AND TIMELINE ALIGNMENT

Marzano (2003) identifies a viable curriculum as a strong indicator of student success. He defines viable as a curriculum that can be reasonably taught within the designated instructional time. Tasking teachers to determine pacing or decide content to be emphasized or de-emphasized is unfair. Teachers must be provided benchmarks by which to gauge progress so that the intended curriculum can be the implemented one. (We discuss benchmark, or common, assessments in depth in Chapter 4.) Mathematics leaders have the role of working with teachers to define benchmarks and to reach consensus on them.

What Are Leaders Expected to Do?

Mathematics leaders should develop a timeline (or pacing guide) for the mathematics program so that teachers can appropriately schedule instructional blocks of time. Curriculum documents need not be perfect before being used. They are "living" documents that are continually revisited, revised, and improved based on experience and research. Adequate time is essential for studying standards and creating curriculum documents. Instructional leaders define scope and sequence, regardless of resources being used, because classroom teachers and students need to recognize mathematical content that is being emphasized during each lesson.

Effective leaders are in constant communication with teachers. Teachers need to feel that they have a voice even though a decision may not always go their way. When decisions are not in line with teacher suggestions, empowered leaders carefully explain their rationale and influential factors. However, in empowered schools the need to overrule teachers' suggestions or recommendations is rare.

Leaders Ensure a Viable Curriculum

The designated curriculum must fit reasonably within an instructional year. And, according to Conzemius and O'Neill (2001), "We also know that children who have the opportunity to learn the content they will be tested on score higher than children who don't learn the material beforehand" (p. 57). Thus, "viable" includes creating a curriculum document that is specific and aligned to future assessment. Initially, this task will require leaders to create foundational documents, including scope, sequence, and timeline, from which to build more comprehensive documents. These three foundational documents are defined as follows:

Scope refers to the depth of mathematics content as it relates to a grade level or course. Age-appropriate concepts and skills are identified, strongly reflecting state standards. The scope of a curriculum document should correlate to test specifications from state-mandated assessments as well as locally produced assessments.

Sequence is the organization and order of objectives identified in the scope. It is designed so that concepts and skills build on one another as students progress through the school year.

Timeline (or *pacing guide*) refers to the estimated blocks of time that teachers will use to teach the objectives identified in the scope and sequence. The timeline also is used as a guideline for common assessments that the district will administer.

With this information as a starting point, mathematics leaders need to initiate conversations with teachers to affirm agreement on definitions and purposes of this part of a curriculum document.

In developing a scope the mathematics teams start with the state-identified content for a particular course or grade. The foundation includes only minimum requirements. For each objective the team needs to decide if the objective is to be introduced, mastered, or reviewed. Team members then organize objectives by clusters of related objectives around mathematical concepts. Skills are attached to objectives that provide an opportunity for application. For instance, recognizing halves and fourths might be combined with lessons on measurement. Students then learn about prime factorization, common factors, common multiples, and finally, how to add and subtract rational numbers. An example of a simple graphic organizer for an instructional unit is shown in Figure 3.1. Of course, some objectives will require routine practice throughout the school year.

With the scope identified, the team should move on to identifying an appropriate sequence for teaching the content. There is no perfect sequence. The team chooses a sequence that members can explain and justify. Often it is easier to sequence by first deciding if the cluster is to be taught in the first or second semester. Following this decision, the clusters can be divided into six- or nine-week blocks, and then further organized by week.

Team members next review the school calendar to provide an estimated time allotment for the clusters. Considering actual teaching time is challenging work. The team needs to anticipate interruptions, such as time for local and state assessments. Looking for additional opportunities to embed skills probably will be necessary.

With an agreed-on scope, sequence, and timeline in place, mathematics leaders can focus on providing guidance-oriented materials to teachers. These are materials that will support teachers in using inclusive instructional approaches and exploring mathematics content in greater depth. The National Research Council (2002) notes, "Instructional materials need to have teacher notes that support teacher's understanding of mathematical concepts, student thinking and student errors, and effective pedagogical supports and techniques" (p. 28). Although such materials may not be comprehensive, they can play a critical role by providing examples for teachers of the scope of mathematics concepts, skills, and practices for students. These materials must match state standards.

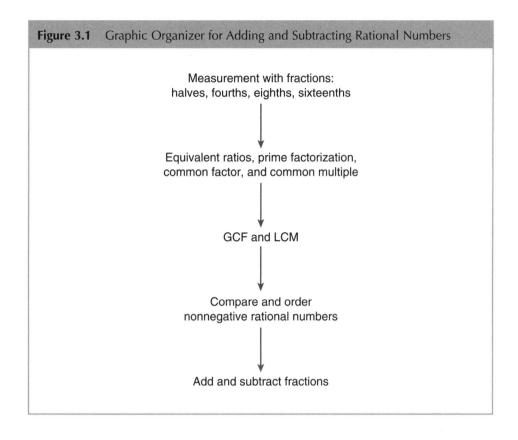

Figure 3.1 Graphic Organizer for Adding and Subtracting Rational Numbers

Measurement with fractions:
halves, fourths, eighths, sixteenths

↓

Equivalent ratios, prime factorization,
common factor, and common multiple

↓

GCF and LCM

↓

Compare and order
nonnegative rational numbers

↓

Add and subtract fractions

Using the scope, sequence, and timeline framework, teacher teams "cement" the units or clusters together into meaningful chunks of instruction. At this point, mathematics teachers usually will see the need to include additional skills and concepts to make the units flow from one to the next in a developmental fashion. While mathematics leaders will want to use available instructional materials in the district, caution must be exercised. State content cannot be forced to fit the district-level materials. On the contrary, district materials must be made to fit the state content constraints. Inappropriate and misaligned materials should be removed from the curriculum guide. This may require mathematics leaders and team members to modify certain instructional materials, bearing in mind that modification is different from substituting one misaligned lesson for another.

Ironically, at times high-profile mathematics educators and professional organizations can get in the way of successful alignment. An example is a professional development program offering suggestions for classroom activities that are not aligned to state standards or local curriculum documents. Teachers return to classrooms with exciting, engaging activities that may be completely misaligned to intended curriculum content. Mathematics leaders need to be attuned to professional development provided to teachers and alert to materials that teachers bring back to classrooms. Open, honest conversations about each element of a curriculum document and its purpose will help teachers participate in a screening process to determine which new approaches, techniques, and materials should be included in an ever-improving document.

Resources That Leaders Can Use

Often, scope can be extracted directly from state standards. Sequence and timeline, however, usually are not provided. Mathematics leaders must take content objectives and place them into concept clusters for learning. Graphic organizers and flow charts are helpful at this stage of the work. Other well-designed curricula also may provide recommendations and suggestions from which to build concept clusters. By clustering learning objectives, teachers connect mathematical skills and concepts. Figure 3.2 shows an example of a unit flowchart. This flowchart shows a unit cluster of Grade 3 objectives relating patterns to multiplication and division facts. Students are to seek out patterns and relations from data on graphs and tables to identify multiplication and division facts.

Numerous resources are available for mathematics leaders to use in aligning to a state curriculum. For example, area mathematics leadership groups can be excellent providers of information and guidance. When possible, leaders can use exemplars from other districts and even other states. Friendships, networks, and professional associations can be used as contacts for working with other mathematics leaders who are going through the same process or have already done so. Working from an established outline often can expedite curriculum alignment work.

RIGOROUS CURRICULUM

The term *rigorous* can be found regularly in today's education literature. Efforts to describe rigorous learning experiences have focused on three principles (Iowa Department of Education, 2005, p. 4):

1. Good teaching is central to improving achievement.

2. Teachers must identify rigorous, well-defined curriculum standards, benchmarks, and corresponding assessments.

3. All stakeholders must hold high expectations for student performance.

How well a curriculum addresses these components, aligns to state standards, assists teachers and students in identifying mathematics concepts,

Figure 3.2 Unit Flowchart Example

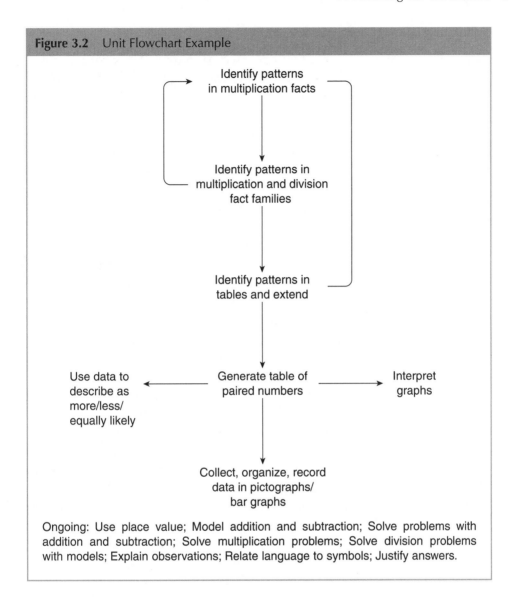

Ongoing: Use place value; Model addition and subtraction; Solve problems with addition and subtraction; Solve multiplication problems; Solve division problems with models; Explain observations; Relate language to symbols; Justify answers.

and provides well-designed lessons determines whether it is "strongly aligned" or "weakly aligned." Among districts there are numerous configurations of available documents. Some districts have curriculum documents, some have curriculum guides, and some have both. However, two general categories emerge. Either a district has adopted or developed a strong supportive curriculum, or it has adopted a weak one. Working within these situations varies.

One resource, developed by Willard R. Daggett, is the Rigor/Relevance Framework™, a tool for school districts to use in addressing these principles. Information about this framework can be found at Daggett's International Center for Leadership in Education website at www.leadered.com.

What Are Leaders Expected to Do?

There is a marked, but often confused, difference between rigor and acceleration. Rigor addresses depth and application of knowledge along with the challenge of problems; acceleration means covering more material in a shorter period of time. While acceleration frequently undermines rigor, rigor can usually accelerate learning. According to the National Research Council (2001), "There is growing evidence that students learn best when they are presented with academically challenging work that focuses on sense making and problem solving as well as skill building" (p. 335). When students are highly engaged in problem solving, thinking, and reflecting on learning, their mathematical knowledge increases, as do retention and transfer. Leaders are expected to facilitate staff discussion about rigor and acceleration, noting how the process standards factor into increased student achievement.

This level of understanding can be achieved only if curriculum materials match the depth of an intended curriculum. Materials also must help teachers and students understand what is meant by "mastery." Mathematics leaders will be expected to provide examples of acceptable student performance.

Leaders cannot assume that an intended curriculum will be the implemented curriculum. Mathematics teachers (like all teachers) do have a curriculum that they teach. This curriculum may be a rich, exploratory, concept-developing curriculum, or it may be a skills-driven, superficial one. In either case, leaders must start with the curriculum currently in practice and strive to improve it.

In creating a curriculum or analyzing a curriculum, there are areas of mathematics proficiency that need to be developed. According to the National Research Council (2001), there are five components of mathematical proficiency:

1. Conceptual understanding—comprehension of mathematical concepts, operations, and relations

2. Procedural fluency—skills in carrying out procedures flexibly, accurately, efficiently, and appropriately

3. Strategic competence—ability to formulate, represent, and solve mathematical problems

4. Adaptive reasoning—capacity for logical thought, reflection, explanation, and justification

5. Productive disposition—habitual inclination to see mathematics as sensible, useful, and worthwhile, coupled with a belief in diligence and one's own efficacy. (p. 116)

Mathematics leaders should understand these components and provide appropriate professional development to staff members so that they, too, understand them.

If mathematics leaders are working with programs, textbooks, or resources that do not entirely meet the NRC proficiencies, then several additional tasks must be completed. First, areas where standards are inappropriately placed, not covered, or covered to insufficient depth should be identified. Teachers must carefully study standards to identify gaps in content and to remove unneeded content. Materials can then be selected to fill in missing or incomplete content. Teachers, usually working in collaborative groups, may need to create replacement units.

Within this framework teachers also will need to develop an estimated time for teaching each objective. Once the scope, sequence, materials, and timeline are developed, the district is poised to offer every student a comparable mathematics curriculum—regardless of which teacher is teaching the course—that is aligned to state standards and meets viability criteria. Additionally, leaders will work with teachers to hone instructional strategies and techniques.

The stronger the initial mathematics curriculum resources are, the better the resulting document will be. Poorly designed, quickly developed, and misaligned instructional materials are difficult to overcome and take extra support from leaders. Devoting extra time and attention to filling holes and creating a document, program, and supplementary materials teachers can depend on is worthwhile.

Even with a strongly aligned curriculum, leaders must carefully evaluate the district mathematics curriculum. If the district has adopted a program that meets specific NRC proficiencies, as described above, then mathematics leaders should check the adopted program to be sure that state standards are addressed and teachers are cognizant of where the standards are embedded in the program. Without a strong curricular foundation, in which everyone concerned is thoroughly familiar with all aspects, instruction and assessment may go awry.

To ensure that state standards are addressed and teachers know where the standards are embedded in the program, leaders can arrange for the mathematics staff, or a subgroup, to study the standards. Anyone involved in working on the district curriculum needs a thorough knowledge of state standards and mathematics content. Based on this information the staff should be able to locate the standards in the program, highlight these standards, and match the depth of the program to the depth of the standards. Finally, the staff should develop a timeline for the program, which will make it possible for teachers to provide appropriate instruction.

Once the curriculum is articulated, leaders recognize the importance of ensuring its use by all. The process begins with distribution and comprehension. We recommend that the appropriate objectives be displayed in the classroom. In many districts and schools, teachers are required to post daily or weekly objectives in prominent places for students to read. Teachers should be encouraged to review the objectives with students periodically and to review concepts that have been taught, thus emphasizing their developmental nature. This approach helps students make the connections in mathematics content and builds on previous knowledge—an excellent teaching strategy (Jensen, 1998). Figure 3.1, provided previously, offers an example of a curriculum flowchart for an instructional unit.

As learning theories and brain research continue to develop, educational pedagogy also continues to evolve. Students learn best when they are able to connect to previous learning and when concepts make sense to them. Mathematics educators for some time have used learning terms such as *meaningful, related, spiraling, concrete to abstract,* and so on. However, curricula have not necessarily been organized to support the intent of these words. By clustering learning objectives, teachers can better connect skills and concepts. Concepts are spiraled so that students consistently revisit concepts and skills in order to launch into new learning. If students fail to grasp critical parts of certain concepts the first time through, they have additional opportunities, because the concepts are regularly revisited.

Leaders also must guide the selection of supplementary materials. Supplements should be chosen to support weak areas in a curriculum and difficult instructional areas. However, sometimes supplements may be added that simply reinforce teachers' comfort and strengths in the curriculum. Leaders need to analyze the areas of content and instruction that are difficult for teachers and students and then push to obtain supplements for these areas.

Resources That Leaders Can Use

NCTM's *Principles and Standards for School Mathematics* (2000) recommends a curriculum document that clearly delineates what students are to learn and emphasizes the developmental nature of mathematics. NCSM's complementary leadership document, *PRIME* (2008), stresses the need to implement the curriculum as designed and to ensure that it is relevant, meaningful, and attained by every student.

Developing and implementing a rigorous curriculum entails lessons that provide students opportunities to explore rich, challenging problems. Students usually have difficulty grasping mathematical depth by listening to a lecture or observing a teacher model a procedure (National Research

Council, 2005, 2004). We take up effective instructional strategies in Chapter 5, which will be useful reading when mathematics leaders are developing or analyzing instructional materials.

To assist mathematics leaders in assessing a curriculum, we believe that the following Curriculum Self-Evaluation (Figure 3.3) may be a useful tool. This is a reflective tool, not to be used like a test but intended to help mathematics leaders highlight critical elements of an articulated curriculum and to identify what might be areas of greatest need.

Figure 3.3

CURRICULUM SELF-EVALUATION

Articulated Curriculum

Directions: The purpose of this self-evaluation is to assist in developing a clearly articulated curriculum document that consists of scope, sequence, timeline, and reference materials. It is a reflective tool to aid the mathematics leader. Rate each item by circling a number with 1 being low and 5 being high.

To what extent

Has your district developed a curriculum guide for mathematics?	1	2	3	4	5
Are objectives detailed and specific?	1	2	3	4	5
Does your curriculum guide recommend instructional strategies?	1	2	3	4	5
Does your curriculum guide contain a scope and sequence?	1	2	3	4	5
Does your scope and sequence contain a timeline?	1	2	3	4	5
Is your district timeline reasonable for the number of mathematics objectives?	1	2	3	4	5
Does your scope and sequence identify state standards?	1	2	3	4	5
Does your scope and sequence identify tested objectives?	1	2	3	4	5
Does your scope and sequence identify introduced skills?	1	2	3	4	5
Does your scope and sequence identify mastered skills?	1	2	3	4	5
Does your scope and sequence identify reinforced skills?	1	2	3	4	5
Is your scope and sequence textbook driven?	1	2	3	4	5
Is your scope and sequence state standards driven?	1	2	3	4	5
Is your scope and sequence organized by objective or unit?	1	2	3	4	5
Does your scope and sequence identify objectives under mathematical concepts?	1	2	3	4	5
Does your scope and sequence identify objectives under "big ideas"?	1	2	3	4	5
Are students taking the advanced courses?	1	2	3	4	5
Are students successful in the courses?	1	2	3	4	5

Two additional questions

Does your timeline separate curriculum by	semester	9-week	6-week	month	week
How many different materials does your scope and sequence reference?	1	2	3	4	5

---

4 Implementing the Curriculum

DEVELOPMENTAL STAGE 2

The mathematics leader ensures that the mathematics curriculum is implemented as designed. A mathematics leader guarantees that

- the developed curriculum plan is followed, and
- student progress is monitored using ongoing assessments.

Mathematics leaders are responsible for facilitating the development of a well-articulated mathematics curriculum—the intended curriculum—as discussed in the previous chapter. Too often, however, after all this work the documents are relegated to a shelf. Possessing an articulated curriculum document is just a first step to student success. The next essential step is to ensure that the curriculum guide is used as planned—the implemented curriculum. Marzano (2003) refers to the written curriculum as the guaranteed curriculum. *Guaranteed* means that a school ensures that classroom teachers address specific content in specific courses or grade levels.

Unless it is monitored, a curriculum cannot be guaranteed and thus successfully implemented by all mathematics teachers. Supportively monitoring implementation of a mathematics curriculum is a major task for mathematics leaders and teachers, but it is only part of the task. Leaders also must ensure that students are learning mathematics content. Regularly scheduled assessments are used to gauge student progress. These assessments need to be rigorous and reflect the established curriculum, complement state mathematics standards, and highlight student understandings and misconceptions.

In this chapter, we will focus on recommendations about how leaders can ensure that the curriculum guide is used as planned and how they can collect data on implementation and its effect on student learning.

CURRICULUM IMPLEMENTATION

Adopting or producing an excellent, aligned curriculum document that goes unused is more than merely a waste of time and energy. The status quo is maintained, the achievement gap is reinforced, and equity is denied. On completion of a curriculum document accompanied by adopted materials, school and district mathematics leaders must take responsibility for ensuring its distribution, comprehension, and use.

What Are Leaders Expected to Do?

A worthwhile curriculum document typically requires changes in traditional classroom approaches to teaching. There probably will be changes in the order and depth of some of the mathematics content. Otherwise, there would have been no reason to create a new document. Such changes will not be effective in classrooms without leaders' intervention and support. Leaders are expected to work with teachers to implement newly developed curricula (Hall & Hord, 2001). They also are expected to work with teachers to ensure that students and parents are aware of the new intended curriculum.

Based on a pacing chart from the scope and sequence, the learning objectives can be rendered visible to students and made available to parents. Teachers should be encouraged to review objectives and concepts with students periodically, taking note of those that have been taught and emphasizing the developmental nature of mathematical concepts and skills.

Leaders Ensure Curriculum Implementation

One of the first challenges for mathematics leaders is to disseminate the correct edition of the curriculum document. This means getting teachers to discard prior documents, which may contain conflicting information. Dating curriculum documents will help ensure that the proper edition is used. Holding a meeting at which teachers "trade in" old documents and obtain the new ones can be helpful.

A way to make the document—or perhaps simply the scope and sequence—generally available both to the school population and to parents is to post it online. Distributing copies at parent-teacher meetings also is worthwhile. Mainly, parents and students need to know about learning expectations; therefore, distributing the entire document probably is not needed. Another useful communications strategy is to send home periodic updates of coming expectations along with students' report cards.

In the classroom, teachers can display and discuss the scope and sequence at the start of each grading period. Mathematics leaders can assist by preparing segments of the document matched to the grading period according to the pacing chart. The more information teachers provide to students about what is to be learned, how skills and concepts are developed and related, and what students must be able to do to show proficiency, the greater the increase in learning is likely to be. Documents such as these usually are developed at the district level with teacher input, produced centrally, and then distributed to teachers to use in their classrooms. At designated intervals, mathematics leaders should plan to hold teacher-team meetings to discuss the scope and sequence, which will reiterate for teachers the important information that needs to be shared with students.

The curriculum document should provide teachers with a list of objectives, a clustered sequence of the objectives, and an estimated time needed to teach the objectives. Teacher teams, directed by a mathematics leader, should study the school calendar and list objectives by date. Teachers then post this information in classrooms or send it home to parents. Doing so gives students important information that they will need if they are absent, and more important, allows teachers to remind students on an ongoing basis what has been learned and how that learning will be used in coming lessons. This procedure can help students get past the disconnected, one-day-at-a-time approach many of them confront in mathematics.

A significant challenge for mathematics leaders can be to get past the barrier of the classroom door. Mathematics leaders need to work to make classrooms more accessible (Schmoker, 1999). Education change occurs when teaching practices become more public and overt. Mathematics leaders must work with teachers, administrators, and other staff to foster understanding about the job of monitoring program implementation—apart from teacher evaluation. This idea is further developed in the next section.

MONITORED IMPLEMENTATION

Curriculum implementation must be monitored (Marzano, 2005). As societal changes are taking place, demographics also are changing. However, changes in instructional methods do not appear to be keeping pace with population shifts. Districts and schools must address the gap in achievement of traditionally underserved populations when compared to other students. Classroom teachers need to employ instructional methods that increase the likelihood of success for *every* student. Teachers need to engage students in practices that focus on sense-making, self-assessment, and reflection (NRC, 2005). Not only do teachers need to use these methods in classrooms, they also need to monitor their practices in ways similar to those they use to monitor student performance. These changes will occur only if mathematics leaders are able to monitor implementation of desired behaviors (Zepeda, 2004).

What Are Leaders Expected to Do?

Mathematics leaders need to monitor classroom activities and the implementation of the intended curriculum through several actions outside of classrooms. Reviewing lesson plans is one such action. Engaging in collaborative lesson planning with teachers is another. These actions can reveal whether high-success instructional strategies are being used and whether the intended mathematics content is being taught. Such external actions, however, cannot substitute for being in classrooms. Classroom visits also are expected of leaders.

Leaders Ensure Curriculum Implementation

Classroom visits are at the heart of successful monitoring. By watching students, mathematics leaders can effectively monitor the effect of every developmental stage. Traditional classroom monitoring tends to focus on teacher behaviors, basically evaluating, not monitoring. Effective monitoring, as we cast it, incorporates techniques for watching what students are doing. The actions of students are key. Students do not learn mathematics from what teachers do, but from what they themselves do in response to teachers' actions.

Classroom visits create challenges for leaders. To begin, school principals have a responsibility to enter classrooms, usually for the purpose of evaluating teachers. In fact, there is a high correlation between successful schools and principals who are instructional leaders (Marzano, 2003). Principals know this. Along with the requirements of No Child Left Behind for greater accountability, principals usually are proactive about classroom observations. So what is the balance between a principal's role in classroom visits and that of a mathematics leader? And how can leaders avoid causing confusion when they also visit classrooms?

Formal school leaders (administrators such as principals) traditionally are trained as efficient managers. A general assumption is that if schools run smoothly, then learning will naturally occur. Research shows that there must be some level of order for learning to happen, but order alone does not ensure learning. For that guarantee, the responsibilities of instructional leadership must be moved to the forefront of education reform efforts, according to Hoachlander, Alt, and Beltranena (2001). Therefore, mathematics leaders need to work in conjunction with principals to promote student learning through implementation of a well-articulated and aligned mathematics curriculum. This is a change from traditional practices and requires making coaching and mentoring available to both principals and mathematics leaders (Hoachlander et al., 2001).

A major factor in this change and a key element of mathematics leadership is leaders intentionally entering classrooms to gather information and to provide support to teachers on an ongoing basis (Williams, 1996). Classroom visits should be designed specifically to assess the degree of program implementation. Managing accurate implementation of an effective program is central to student success.

A substantial challenge for school principals—and an area in which they will need assistance from mathematics leaders—is recognizing that entering classrooms to manage program implementation is different from conducting teacher evaluations. Instructional leaders should clearly recognize and be able to articulate differences between evaluative classroom observations and supportive classroom visits in order to avoid crossing the line of authority. Following are some key distinctions.

Classroom observations

- are part of a formal teacher evaluation process,
- gather data about specific teachers,
- often are state- or district-required and last 45 minutes or more,
- include documentation that is placed in teachers' files and may be positive or negative, and
- are designed to rate teachers against an identified norm of behavior.

Classroom visits

- are used to gather information about types of instruction and degree of curriculum implementation with the purpose of rating schools, not individuals;
- are nonevaluative in terms of observing teachers;
- look for trends and patterns in cumulative, rather than individual, data; and
- seldom exceed 15 minutes in length and usually last only three to seven minutes.

Nothing undermines innovation more quickly or completely than treating monitoring for program implementation as if it were teacher evaluation (Love, 2004). Teachers need time, encouragement, and feedback to change behaviors. Mathematics leaders, for the most part, do not evaluate teachers. If mathematics leaders compile data that end up in teachers' files, trust and cooperation are likely to be dramatically reduced and change efforts can grind to a halt.

A couple of reasons support short visits to monitor implementation. First, the visit is not to evaluate teachers, traditionally done during longer observation periods. Therefore, short visits reinforce the idea that teachers are not being evaluated. Second, leaders use short visits to take a "snapshot" of a program, monitoring as many classes as possible over a relatively brief time span. The focus is on what is happening in these few minutes in classrooms and what is happening in this school during mathematics classes.

Yet another rationale for monitoring program implementation is for leaders to ask, "What percent of teachers are ready, willing, and able to adopt the innovation or program?" Leaders should realize that a critical mass of teacher support is necessary for change to occur, and peer pressure can be an effective means for increasing the use of an innovation or program (Williams, 1996). If a majority of teachers does not support and use the adopted curriculum, then a positive effect on student learning will not be achieved.

Consequently, garnering teacher support is a key responsibility, and it is not likely to come by way of negative feedback from a formal observation. Attempts by principals to "hammer" implementation compliance through formal evaluation processes are never well received and most assuredly will not empower the mathematics staff. Negative approaches by principals will place mathematics leaders in an awkward situation—caught between supporting and defending principals, teachers, and the mathematics program—and should be avoided at all cost.

With support from teachers—garnered through effective classroom visits and ensuing professional conversations—positive change will have the greatest likelihood of success. According to Reeves (2004) teachers' intrinsic motivation is activated when actions are connected to student learning. Classroom visits send a clear, consistent message of expectations and demonstrate empathy for teachers and support for the change process in classrooms.

Resources That Leaders Can Use

Generic checklists cannot target specific mathematics expectations and may actually interfere with effective classroom instruction. Teachers may not understand terms on the form or may try to incorporate every item in every lesson. Thus, it makes sense to customize a form to fit the curriculum. Mathematics leaders should enter classrooms with a plan to monitor specific behaviors that teachers have helped to identify. Two starting points are provided, one for students (Figure 4.1), another for teachers (Figure 4.2). Both are designed to be customized so that teachers, principals, and mathematics leaders can work together without blurring lines between support and evaluation.

Mathematics leaders, with assistance from administrators and teachers, should be able to develop a customized classroom visit form easily. Including teachers in the process ensures that the correct instructional strategies are included and assists in clarifying the terms used on the form. Customizing the form also allows leaders to do the following:

- Balance the role between leader and manager
- Support alignment among the written, taught, and tested curricula
- Promote a philosophy of continuous improvement
- Move schools from being institutions of teaching to becoming institutions of learning
- Be nonevaluative and focused on improvement
- Promote teacher involvement in the improvement process
- Target specific curriculum and strategies critical to the district
- Establish clear expectations for students and teachers

Mathematics leaders should work toward identifying a manageable number of skills for teachers to master that can do the following:

- Be adapted with time and expertise
- Align to professional development
- Provide a sense of accomplishment
- Provide accurate feedback data
- Open lines of communication
- Show empathy for and understanding of teachers

Four steps are needed to customize a classroom-visit tally:

1. A committee of school leaders, mathematics teachers, and central-office support staff carefully studies the adopted mathematics program and materials. Their goal is to identify recommended strategies for teachers and behaviors for students that are embedded in the program. Committee members look at grouping students, clarifying objectives, using technology, and using manipulatives.

Figure 4.1

Classroom-Visit Tally: Students

School: _____

Date: _____ Grade or Course: _____

Students are	Classroom				
	CR1	CR2	CR3	CR4	CR5
Discussing mathematics.					
Answering questions that extend mathematics (What if . . . ? What would happen . . . ?).					
Demonstrating understanding (oral, written, hands-on).					
Using a variety of tools in a lesson.					
Working collaboratively in pairs.					
Working collaboratively in small groups.					
Sharing/explaining their thinking.					
Using technology (calculators, computers).					
Engaging in classroom activities.					
Investigating/exploring mathematical concepts.					

Comments

Classroom 1:

_____

_____

Classroom 2:

_____

_____

Classroom 3:

_____

_____

Classroom 4:

_____

_____

Classroom 5:

_____

_____

Figure 4.2

Classroom-Visit Tally: Teachers

School: _____

Date: _____ Grade or Course: _____

Teachers are	Classroom				
	CR1	CR2	CR3	CR4	CR5
Discussing mathematics.					
Encouraging discussion about mathematics (students to students).					
Asking higher-order questions.					
Asking probing and scaffolding questions.					
Providing engaging activities.					
Using a variety of tools in lessons.					
Using technology (calculators, computers).					
Providing wait time.					
Using grouping strategies: • Pairs (think/pair/share, reciprocal) • Small groups (round robin, jigsaw, lineups)					
Teaching with multiple representations.					
Providing problem solving/exploration experiences.					
Monitoring interactions (moving around the room, etc.).					

Comments

Classroom 1:

_____

_____

Classroom 2:

_____

_____

Classroom 3:

_____

_____

Classroom 4:

_____

_____

Classroom 5:

_____

_____

2. Committee members review the professional development that has occurred within the last several years. Are there strategies from the training that are not on the current list? If so, they add these strategies.

3. Members reflect on the school district's expectations or beliefs. Has the district mandated certain activities, such as journal writing, silent reading, calculators, or an emphasis on problem solving or real-world applications? They include any of these activities that are not already listed.

4. Committee members determine the most important elements of the completed list. These are items that make an adopted program actually function. In other words, if these strategies are not used, then the program is not being implemented to any degree of fidelity and therefore will be unlikely to produce appreciable improvement in student learning. These items are highlighted. Additional items placed on the list will be optional and included by committee consensus. The committee should work to hold the listed teacher behaviors or student actions to one page each so that a front/back form can be printed.

Mathematics leaders should retain the compiled list of strategies for future reference. Then the classroom-visit tally should be adjusted over time to meet new expectations. As proficiency and a level of comfort are achieved, some strategies will become routine and new ones can be placed on the list.

By gathering data on the classroom-visit tallies, leaders can help teachers recognize which instructional strategies they most often use and the level of student engagement that results. They also can compare the strategies noted to the list of recommended strategies in the adopted curriculum. In a two-minute "walk-through," only a few strategies are noted. The compilation of strategies over a window of time and multiple classrooms makes the data worthwhile for determining the degree of program implementation. Using achievement data, leaders can compare the degree of program implementation to the level of student achievement. Provided in a supportive way that acknowledges efforts of teachers, these accountability data will motivate and empower teachers (Reeves, 2004).

Following are things mathematics leaders need to keep in mind when using a classroom-visit tally:

- The forms identify teacher actions and student actions. No teacher names are attached to the form. Data are gathered and analyzed by subject (such as fifth-grade mathematics) or course (such as Algebra I).

- Visit results are collected during a set timeframe (perhaps a one- or two-week period). While collecting data, staff members decide the amount of time to be allotted per classroom and then follow the schedule as closely as possible.
- Completing the forms while in classrooms is not advisable because this routine is a characteristic of evaluation. Visitors enter classrooms, observe for two to seven minutes, and then leave. Once in the hall, they check items and record any other information. Then they immediately enter another classroom and repeat the process. The visitor's name may be added if there are multiple observers.
- Visitors avoid skewing data by not confining visits to the first or last few minutes of every class. The idea is to gather snapshots of classroom behavior at different times.
- Completed forms are stored until all data are collected and analyzed. Mathematics leaders should encourage as many staff participants as possible to be involved in collecting the data. However, staff members conducting visits need to be aware of the "halo effect"—the tendency to observe based on personal opinions or past experiences. If a behavior is not observed, it is not recorded, in spite of the desire to give the observed individual the benefit of the doubt.

The tally process removes the "intimidation" factor that some mathematics teachers use to influence principals who lack in-depth knowledge of mathematics content. The tally process blunts the common notion that goes, "Since the administrator does not know mathematics, he or she cannot truly supervise teachers."

Using the tallies is necessarily a fairly formal, structured process. An informal variation is simply to collect data on effective strategies by mathematics leaders visiting classrooms specifically looking for indicators of the desired strategies and logging what they observe on "scratch paper." For example, if a mathematics leader has been assisting teachers with planning lessons that are more engaging for students, they may have discussed grouping strategies or having students work with a partner. The lessons have been developed, but are they being presented as planned? Leaders can conduct short, informal classroom visits, looking for these specific strategies.

In this case two quick data points are collected:

1. Are the instructional strategies occurring at this moment?
2. If yes, what are the strategies?

As in formal visits using the classroom-visit tally, data are gathered to support implementation of desired instructional strategies. Using these data, leaders are able to interject positive comments into the next planning session and ask critical questions about strategy selection and use.

Although we use scratch paper to convey that this is a process without formal documentation being gathered or used, mathematics leaders should keep several things in mind:

- Teachers should know about this process and what a leader is doing.
- Teachers should know how the information will be used.
- No formal record is compiled, although the leader may keep his or her notes.
- Data are not shared outside the group without the group's permission.

The information is valuable for leaders and teachers. If strategies are being planned but not used, the issues need to be explored. If some strategies are being overused, then additional information or training can be introduced to a planning group. Finally, as with the formal process, teachers and leaders may discover a communication problem. Teachers may think they are using the strategies, while leaders do not.

MONITORED PROGRESS

Mathematics leaders should start with assessments from locally adopted materials. Depending on the quality of these materials the assessments may or may not be useful. However, a review of these materials will be beneficial for future work with benchmark assessments. Leaders also will need to draw on state assessments available to the public as well as practice tests and review resources. Leaders must work with teachers to identify desired student actions that increase learning. Mathematics leaders will need to use previous professional development work and other statements to ascertain the philosophy of the district about student learning.

There are multiple references to assessments in this book. Mathematics leaders and teachers need to offer and use a wide array of assessment measures. One such approach is the benchmark assessment. Benchmark assessments, often referred to as common assessments, are only one of many types of assessments. Following the development and implementation of an aligned curriculum, leaders work with teachers to establish benchmarks. Benchmark assessments align to the sequence document and are administered at regular intervals, such as every six or nine weeks. Alignment of the assessment items to the mathematics content is the goal, because alignment directly affects student learning (Marzano, 2003).

What Are Leaders Expected to Do?

Benchmark assessments are defined as tests that are regularly administered within a designated window of time across the same course. These tests are usually multiple choice and easily graded. Mathematics leaders work with teachers in conducting item analyses and preparing data that are available to principals. Figure 4.3 provides a simple analysis of an open response item.

Figure 4.3 Example of Item Analysis

Grade 8 Open Response

Total 10 Item Test: 69.2% passing with 80% proficiency (18/26)

Item 7: A student wants to have $590 in the bank at the end of the year. How much money, to the nearest cent, should she put in the bank if the simple interest rate is 3%?

State Standard: Solve problems by computing simple and compound interest.

Item Analysis

- 13 students correctly answered the question ($572.82).
- 3 students responded: Multiply .03 × 590, so $17.70 should be invested.
- 6 students responded: Multiply .03 × 590, and subtract from $590. So $572.80 should be invested.
- 4 students responded: Multiply .03 × 590, and add to $590. So $643.10 should be invested.

In effective schools, according to Spillane and colleagues (2002),

The principal has led the effort to run test-score analysis on data provided by the district so that teachers can chart the progress of school-level reforms by subject area and grade level. These leadership strategies have shifted the import of test-score data within the school's improvement agenda—transforming the body of student outcome data from something the district simply demands to a tool that the school fully expects to use. (p. 738)

While benchmark assessments are one of the most effective practices that successful administrators regularly employ, such assessments often are met with concerns from teachers (Reeves, 2006). Mathematics leaders must be aware of and sensitive to these concerns. For instance, some teachers may want clarity and assurance on the following questions:

- How are data to be used?
- Who has access to the data?
- Are the data evaluative of teacher performance?
- Is the time assessing worth the classroom time needed?
- Are the data used to inform instruction?
- Who is responsible for grading and analyzing the data?
- How are tests created, stored, and used?

Mathematics leaders are expected to review and analyze benchmark assessments. These assessments should validate leaders' expectations that the developed curriculum is being taught. By insisting that assessments be analyzed, mathematics leaders take active steps to ensure student learning. This message that student learning is key must be consistent throughout the process. Learning expectations, classroom visits, and benchmark assessments are all intended to help teachers improve instruction and increase student learning. Data are used to help teachers improve, to refine the curriculum, and to provide teachers and students opportunities to reflect on learning. These processes are never intended to be punitive.

Mathematics leaders are expected to use data to give feedback to students, something that often is overlooked. The most common practice is for data to be individualized, private, and given as merely a grade. Individual students or groups of students certainly should not be identified or singled out; however, students can learn a great deal by reviewing cumulative data. This is especially true for analyzing error patterns and distracters. Students need to reflect on their learning (NRC, 2000). They also need to be encouraged to perform well as a class.

Leaders Ensure Learning Progress

Creating a valid and reliable assessment item is much more difficult than it would first appear. For this reason, mathematics leaders need to be patient and expect evolution of the assessment items to occur over time. Mathematics leaders should expect many trial-and-error approaches and modifications. Though assessments will improve over time, every assessment can provide useful data. However, we strongly caution mathematics leaders not to base mandates or edicts or draw conclusions from any one version of an assessment. Data patterns over time are the best indicators of areas or items in need of adjustment.

A first source for assessment items is the adopted instructional materials from publishers. Published materials usually have undergone years of refinement and been tried in practice. Teachers often are comfortable with these items because they have used them for unit tests. If possible, the best approach is a gradual one. Teachers initially may be reluctant to administer these types of assessments. Mathematics leaders should accept this and strive to include common items for group analysis. As assessment items are used and discussed, teachers will become more astute about the usefulness of certain items.

A second source of items is any public state assessment document, such as training manuals, sample items, practice items, or, when available, actual released tests that have entered the public domain. Many states place copies of released tests online. Some states, even though they do not release actual tests, make public a variety of practice and sample items that can be adapted for classroom use.

Mathematics leaders may need to observe district regulations that control the writing, distribution, grading, and analysis of benchmark assessments. If these regulations are not in place, mathematics leaders will need to work with teachers to decide how the tests will be used. Some questions include the following:

- Are the tests distributed by the district or handled within individual schools?
- How are privacy and confidentiality to be handled?
- Are test results checked at the district or school level?
- Do the assessments employ a pre/post format?
- How are data organized, analyzed, and reported?
- Who receives data, and what is done with the data afterward?

These are important questions. As long as district policies on student confidentiality are observed, benchmarks can be effective in many arrangements. The most important point is that teachers must be dealt with honestly and openly. Mathematics leaders must broker assessment-related conversations between administrators and teachers. Mathematics leaders usually will not make all of the decisions, but they can keep teachers informed when principals and others make assessment-related decisions.

In working with benchmark assessments a balance must be found between what students need to know and what they are expected to do. In effective instruction, assessments often can be useful as part of an introduction to a unit. Viewing and discussing outcome assessments give students clearer expectations for what demonstrating competence looks like. Teachers and mathematics leaders must decide if this discussion will be drawn from actual assessment items. In most textbooks, chapter and unit tests are included. If assessments will contain these items, then they certainly are readily available to students.

Mathematics leaders also will need to work with teachers to determine how the marking of tests will be done. Scoring needs to be as easy as possible. Data are needed promptly if they are to inform coming instruction. Students need data to help them self-assess their learning and perhaps to alert them about a need to participate in tutoring or some other learning intervention program. If a benchmark is in a multiple-choice format on an answer sheet, for example, classroom teachers can quickly mark the assessment for their classroom and then provide the score/answer sheets to mathematics leaders for school and district cumulative analysis. The school or district should provide assessment scores by teacher or by classroom, plus item analysis by classroom, school, and district.

School administrators, mathematics leaders, and teachers also need to analyze data by ethnicity and gender. Patterns of bias must be considered. When grading and analyzing data, educators must be alert to identify whether a particular group of students is consistently answering certain items incorrectly. Leaders also must ensure that language is not an issue, nor should students' out-of-school experiences be significant factors in the assessments. Cultural sensitivity is extremely important and clearly related to equity considerations. Analysis should ensure that every student is learning the required mathematics content and skills, and if they are not, that they are offered appropriate intervention to remedy the situation. When student progress is monitored over time, learning can be demonstrated. But it also will allow for appropriate and timely remediation to occur.

The diagnostics for students should include distracter analysis, which involves showing students sample problems and asking about their reasoning for a particular answer choice. This type of analysis can be a powerful teaching aid. Students need to reflect on their thinking and reasoning. By discussing error patterns from group scores, students are required to think about their thinking, something known as metacognition. Analyzing error patterns also allows teachers to gain insight into their students' reasoning. Teachers may ask for student input that will help ensure that future lessons are more successful in helping students respond correctly.

According to the National Council of Teachers of Mathematics (2000), "Assessments should support the learning of important mathematics and furnish useful information to both teachers and students" (p. 22). Benchmark assessments are not the end of assessment but merely one piece of a complex process. Teachers who have been expected to write and administer their own tests, grade them in isolation, and return grades to students are going to need time and support to transition to the process of team analysis of assessment data. A first step is administering common assessment items and reviewing the data by item analysis. With this information teachers will be able to make more informed decisions about instructional practices and modify instruction accordingly. Once this process is mastered, teachers will be prepared to broaden the scope of assessment types.

Finally, leaders must be aware of subtle messages that are sent by assessments to teachers, students, and parents about the type of mathematics that is valued and important. Although they are a good place to start, benchmark assessments must never be *the* assessment approach. Students, as well as teachers, may assume that a multiple-choice test format is the one that is most important and provides the most accurate information. This assumption is unfair to students who do not respond well to multiple-choice tests. Various assessment approaches, including observing, listening, using engaging problems, working in groups, responding to open-ended questions, and using rubrics, projects, or interviews, should all used.

Resources That Leaders Can Use

Unless mathematics leaders have a rather large budget with unlimited leeway in spending, they will need to rely on local resources. Leaders may wish to contact surrounding districts to see what is currently being used in their assessment programs. Particular care should be taken to ask about problems and pitfalls that should be avoided.

Benchmark assessments can have a positive effect on student learning, but mathematics leaders should not rush to get them in place. Aligning assessment items to content takes time and effort. Mistakes will be made and poor-quality items will be selected if the process is hurried. Mathematics leaders and teachers generally are not trained to develop reliable and valid test items. For this reason, gathering teachers together during the summer—an all-too-common procedure—to write the benchmark tests from scratch should be discouraged.

Selecting assessment items is difficult, but leaders do have options. As mentioned earlier, they can start with assessments they currently have in materials, resources, and textbooks. Rewriting and adjusting assessment items is easier than starting cold. They can carefully review sample items offered by their state. Actual items may not be available, but sample items can serve as valuable models from which teachers and leaders can construct items.

To assist mathematics leaders in establishing an implemented curriculum, we believe that the following Curriculum Self-Evaluation (Figure 4.4) may be useful. It parallels the self-evaluation we included in Chapter 3. Like that checklist, it is a reflective tool, not to be used like a test but intended to help mathematics leaders highlight critical elements of an implemented curriculum and to identify what might be areas of need.

Figure 4.4

CURRICULUM SELF-EVALUATION

Implemented Curriculum

Directions: The purpose of this self-evaluation is to assist in implementing a curriculum document and to measure progress using benchmark assessments. It is a reflective tool to aid the mathematics leader. Rate each item by circling a number with 1 being low and 5 being high.

To What Extent . . .

Are the teachers following the district curriculum?	1	2	3	4	5
Are teachers using the designated materials?	1	2	3	4	5
Are teachers using the designated strategies?	1	2	3	4	5
Has the district developed benchmark assessments?	1	2	3	4	5
Do benchmark assessments contain a timeline?	1	2	3	4	5
Is the number of objectives in district assessments reasonable?	1	2	3	4	5
Do assessment results identify the state standards?	1	2	3	4	5
Do assessment results identify the tested objectives?	1	2	3	4	5
Do assessments include introduced skills?	1	2	3	4	5
Do assessments include mastered skills?	1	2	3	4	5
Do assessments include reinforced skills?	1	2	3	4	5
Is assessment textbook driven?	1	2	3	4	5
Is assessment state standards driven?	1	2	3	4	5
Is implementation of the curriculum being monitored?	1	2	3	4	5
Are classroom visits occurring?	1	2	3	4	5

Two additional questions

Are your assessments given by	semester	9-week	6-week	month	week
How many different materials does your scope and sequence reference?	1	2	3	4	5

5 Incorporating Effective Instructional Strategies

At this point in the process, mathematics leaders will have initiated several important steps toward effecting change. In previous developmental stages, we suggested that leaders begin the process of engaging and empowering staff by opening channels of communication and establishing clear expectations. We then recommended that leaders work to establish a rigorous, viable, and aligned mathematics curriculum that is challenging and achievable for all students. Once a curriculum has been articulated, leaders will work to ensure implementation of the curriculum as intended. As soon as these initiatives are under way, mathematics leaders should next be prepared to work on incorporating effective instructional practices into classrooms.

Mathematics leaders must understand the relationship between content and effective instructional strategies. Teachers should know numerous strategies and be fluent in using them. Matching an appropriate strategy or group of strategies to the needs of students is paramount for academic achievement. Fluency with effective, research-supported strategies helps leaders embed strategies in the curriculum, select additional strategies as needed, and screen supplemental materials for desired practices. Using an articulated curriculum, mathematics leaders can readily use data to determine the effectiveness of various strategies and support teachers' efforts at matching content to instruction.

Effective teaching requires the use of various forms of instruction. Increases in student learning are directly related to strategic choices made by mathematics teachers (Marzano, 2003). Appropriate strategies can increase learning for all students. But there also are specific instructional strategies that target particular needs. And teachers should to be able to move fluidly from effective, global strategies to intentional, targeted ones. Leaders must understand how such strategies interrelate and encourage and support classroom teachers in applying these strategies.

INCORPORATING EFFECTIVE INSTRUCTIONAL STRATEGIES FOR ALL

Global strategies should reflect current research on best practices. Some researchers—for example, Marzano (2001)—provide lists of instructional strategies that have been shown to be effective. Such lists provide a starting point for mathematics leaders.

Two global strategies, for example, emerge from research and seem to anchor a number of other, related strategies:

1. Student collaboration in the form of teamwork (Starnes, 2006; Wagner, 2005; Marzano, 2001)

2. Group-worthy problems (Boaler, 2006)

These two lesson approaches provide multiple opportunities for incorporating additional strategies that assist students in learning meaningful mathematics, such as generating and testing hypotheses, summarizing, and taking notes. Strategies also can incorporate dialoguing at high levels and making meaning. If students are encouraged to show their work and explain their thinking, then teachers can reinforce students' efforts and provide recognition (Marzano, 2001). Effective student grouping requires teachers to refine their questioning skills and use of prompts and cues.

STUDENT COLLABORATION
IN THE FORM OF TEAMWORK

Regardless of age, students bring to school an understanding of how the world works. Their ideas are undoubtedly incomplete and may be erroneous, but nonetheless they constitute each student's frame of reference (National Research Council, 2000). In mathematics, for example, students may have a feel for numbers and counting; they probably know selected shapes; they might understand fractional sharing by dividing a candy bar with a friend. To learn with new understanding, students must relate new learning to prior understandings. But if incomplete understandings or misconceptions are not addressed, then students will build their mathematics learning on faulty beliefs. For example, some students hold a common misconception about how to add fractions. They add across numerators and denominators ($\frac{3}{4} + \frac{2}{3} = \frac{5}{7}$, where numerators 3 + 2 = 5, and denominators 4 + 3 = 7). This error can persist in spite of multiple corrections. Identifying such misconceptions and determining students' levels of understanding of concepts soon to be taught are two important instructional tasks. Teachers need to find ways to uncover and correct misconceptions (National Research Council, 2000).

Unfortunately, in most classrooms the number of students makes in-depth questioning of individuals virtually impossible. Of course, verbally asking students questions is not the only avenue for checking and monitoring understanding. Teachers also ask students to do exercises that require written explanations. Both approaches are commendable and strongly encouraged, but they simply are not sufficient. Furthermore, students need time to think and to process information in order to make their depth of understanding visible to themselves as well as to teachers (National Research Council, 2000).

A strong rationale for collaborative learning experiences is that students thereby gain sufficient time to think about what they are learning. By engaging in shared activities, students are able to connect their current learning to previous learning. They have time to recall previous learning and process information related to new concepts being taught. Being able to discuss one's thinking increases performance, improves retention, and assists with future knowledge transfer (Kaser et al., 2001). Sharing their thinking with others also helps individual students catch and correct misunderstandings early.

Students do not learn mathematics by listening and imitating; they must be actively engaged (National Research Council, 1989, 2004). "Students enjoy and exert more effort when they are active participants than when they are passive" (National Research Council, 2004, p. 50).

Active engagement is greatly increased when learning activities allow students to work in pairs or small groups. Collaborative activities that require sharing and meaningful interactions in which students explain and justify their reasoning, defend their conclusions, and explore alternative solutions are highly engaging (National Research Council, 2004).

Collaboration: Evidence and Indicators

To achieve a desirable level of participation and processing time—and therefore learning—teachers need to give students opportunities to work in collaborative teams on challenging assignments. When students work on shared problems and discuss possible solutions, teachers are better able to listen to students' reasoning and to target specific, probing questions as needed.

What is effective collaboration and, just as important, what is it not? Let's consider what collaboration is not:

- Independent seatwork while seated in clusters
- Skill practice
- Having the "smartest" student complete the assignment for the group

Effective collaboration involves students doing the following things:

- Shared, multi-step problems requiring gathering and organizing data
- Mathematics tasks that most students could not or would not do independently
- Mathematics tasks that can be solved in multiple ways
- Mathematics tasks that require multiple representations of number or other data (tabular, graphical, algebraic, pictorial, written)

The two lists that follow can be used to guide mathematics leaders. When mathematics leaders visit classrooms, they should look for several indicators of effective student collaboration. For example, students should be

- Talking, sharing, and doing mathematics;
- Sharing task assignments;
- Gathering and organizing data;
- Using mathematical tools (charts, calculators, manipulatives);
- Conjecturing and supporting their ideas;
- Listening and reflecting on other students' suggestions;
- Compiling their findings into presentation formats; and
- Sharing their findings and solutions with the class.

In classrooms where effective collaboration is taking place, the teacher should be observed

- Circulating throughout the room;
- Asking clarifying and probing questions;
- Focusing on both groups and individual students while maintaining a whole-classroom perspective;
- Being aware of time and pacing; and
- Using his or her presence to maintain order.

These lists are not intended to be comprehensive. Mathematics leaders will need to verify, delete, and add elements to suit the needs of their situations.

What Are Leaders Expected to Do?

Mathematics leaders first must determine teachers' current use of and level of understanding about student collaboration. Conversations with teachers are imperative. As noted earlier, teachers are engaged and empowered to participate in the change process. Then leaders can gather and share information, such as the sort we have outlined above.

Classroom visits are a way to gather information about teachers' understanding and use of collaborative teams for instruction. Together, leaders and teachers can identify effective team activities, and teachers can try some strategies.

Two important considerations arise in introducing students to teaming. First, students need to be trained to work in collaborative groups. Classroom teachers should set clear expectations for students that emphasize behaviors and results. Students need to be encouraged to share their thoughts as well as information, to work with other students on assigned tasks, and to reach consensus. Teachers can help students practice group work by engaging classes in several short collaborative activities. Second, teachers need to be proactive about trial and error when it comes to using collaboration. Failed strategies should be discussed, but such conversations should be focused on what worked, alternatives that might have worked, and what to try next.

Many activities and problems are readily adaptable to collaborative teamwork. However, not every problem is group worthy. Group-worthy problems are those that normally would be too difficult, too complex, or too time consuming for an individual student to tackle successfully. Following are two examples. The first is adapted from Balka (2002); the second from Hull, Balka, and Harbin Miles (2009).

EXAMPLE 1

Conjecturing and Reasoning About Geometric Solids

(High School Geometry)

Setting the Stage

Students have been constructing, naming, and drawing two-dimensional representations of various three-dimensional figures. The first task is for collaborative teams to identify some of the important attributes of these figures, listing these terms on the chalkboard, white board, or chart paper. (Terms will include *prism, pyramid, vertices, faces, edges, base, apex,* and *lateral faces.*) Next the teacher should say, "Today we want to explore conjectures. A conjecture is like a guess. It describes relationships among mathematical concepts. For this activity, I want you to make conjectures about relationships between the name of the figure and the number of vertices, faces, and edges."

Exploration

Next the teacher asks students to work in pairs, with one student constructing a solid and the other recording information. Then students should reverse roles. The teacher should distribute several Geofix™ shapes to each pair.

   The teacher then gives each student two activity sheets. One is labeled "Vertices, Faces, and Edges for Prisms;" the other "Vertices, Faces, and Edges for Pyramids." The sheet for prisms is partially illustrated below:

Name of Prism	Number of Vertices (V)	Number of Faces (F)	Number of Edges (E)
Triangular			
Rectangular			
Pentagonal			
Hexagonal			

Summary

After all groups have completed the activity sheet, they should discuss their findings. The teacher then asks the groups for their conjectures about the relationships and discusses how to use the variables to develop algebraic expressions for the total number of vertices, faces, and edges:

(Continued)

(Continued)

Prisms

$V = 2 \times$ Name

$F =$ Name $+ 2$

$E = 3 \times$ Name

Pyramids

$V =$ Name $+ 1$

$F =$ Name $+ 1$

$E = 2 \times$ Name

Effective Collaboration in Action

During the exploration phase of the lesson, students work as partners. One student constructs a prism or pyramid; the other student counts and records the number of vertices, faces, and edges of the figure. Once all columns have been completed, the students together examine patterns in the tables and attempt to make conjectures about the data.

After students have determined the relationships that exist between the names of prisms or pyramids and the three attributes, they present information (clues) using the relationships. Finally, the teacher asks students to construct the three-dimensional figure with Geofix™ shapes. An example might be a hexagonal prism, which has 12 vertices.

Source: Balka, Don S. Exploring Geometry with Geofix. Rowley, MA: Didax, 2002, pp. 42–46.

EXAMPLE 2

Finding Equivalent Fractions

(Elementary Mathematics)

Setting the Stage

The teacher takes a sheet of blank paper and asks students to describe it. After listening to the responses, the teacher folds the paper in half and asks students to describe it now. The teacher asks, "How can I label the sections?" (Each is one half.) The teacher again folds the paper in half (fourths). Opening up the paper, the teacher asks, "What can you tell me about the sections of the paper now? How can I label the sections this time? What do you notice about the section I labeled one half? Does it have another name? (two fourths)." The teacher explains, "One-half and two-fourths are equivalent fractions. Why do you think mathematicians named them equivalent fractions?" The teacher then establishes collaborative teams. Younger students may need to work in pairs until they have more experience collaborating, but the teacher's goal should be to have students work in larger groups of three or four students.

Exploration

The teacher gives each group four paper strips of the same length and asks, "What do you know about the strips?" (They are the same length.) Next, the teacher asks each student to pick up one strip and instructs the group leaders to label their strip as 1:

1

The teacher then asks the student to the right of the leader in each group to fold his or her strip in half and asks, "What would you label each section?" (one half):

$\frac{1}{2}$	$\frac{1}{2}$

Next, the teacher says, "Talk in your group about how you would find fourths." Following the group discussion, the teacher instructs the students to fold the third strip into fourths:

$\frac{1}{4}$	$\frac{1}{4}$	$\frac{1}{4}$	$\frac{1}{4}$

Finally, the teacher says, "Now fold the last strip into eighths and label each section:"

$\frac{1}{8}$	$\frac{1}{8}$	$\frac{1}{8}$	$\frac{1}{8}$	$\frac{1}{8}$	$\frac{1}{8}$	$\frac{1}{8}$	$\frac{1}{8}$

Holding up strips labeled with halves and fourths, the teacher discusses the equivalent fractions $\frac{1}{2} = \frac{2}{4}$ and writes them on the board.

$\frac{1}{2}$	$\frac{1}{2}$

$\frac{1}{4}$	$\frac{1}{4}$	$\frac{1}{4}$	$\frac{1}{4}$

The teacher asks, "Why are the fractions equivalent?" (The strips are the same length.) Next, the teacher issues the lesson challenge: "Your group task is, first, to find and record as many equivalent fractions as you can and, second, to organize your findings in a chart."

(Continued)

(Continued)

As the groups work, the teacher will need to be sure that students are organizing data in a way that makes sense to them and are finding equivalent fractions with numerators greater than 1. The teacher also should make sure that the fraction strips are being shared.

Summary

Teachers should have a discussion in which students consider related questions, such as these: Did you find $\frac{1}{2} = \frac{2}{4}$ and $\frac{2}{4} = \frac{4}{8}$? What do you notice about the relationship between numerators and denominators? Are there other fractions besides the ones we used? Can you name some of them? How could we use the paper strips to find them?

Effective Collaboration in Action

Students work together to ensure that the fraction strips are labeled correctly. Even though each student is responsible for a strip, the group is watching carefully for accuracy. After the strips are labeled, one student holds his or her strip on the table, and the others compare their strips to find equivalent fractions. One student records the findings, or each may record them individually. In an effective group, students quickly realize that they must agree on an organizational method to both find equivalent fractions and record their findings. Students should discover that keys to effective collaboration include

- sharing ideas,
- recording information on a common sheet,
- sharing the fraction strips,
- allowing others to participate in finding an equivalent fraction.

Collaboration can serve many purposes. When students work together, they often are more engaged, interested, and motivated than when they work by themselves. Collaboration also assists teachers in catching and correcting students' misconceptions.

USING GROUP-WORTHY PROBLEMS

A higher level of collaboration can be achieved by using group-worthy problems, which are key to enriched student collaboration (Boaler, 2006). Most students want to be challenged. Tasks with insufficient challenge are boring and do not help students learn meaningful mathematics. On the other hand, tasks that are too difficult distract students from the mathematics they need to learn and give them the feeling that they are not adept at doing mathematics (National Research Council, 2000). Group-worthy problems balance difficulty and address appropriate learning objectives.

Mathematics leaders can best encourage the use of group-worthy problems by initially scheduling planning sessions with teachers in which an instructional plan can be developed. Mathematics leaders also can schedule and participate in reflective activities with teachers that discuss the effects of lessons that incorporate group-worthy problems. These types of discussions allow leaders and teachers to review evidence of learning by looking at student products that result from a lesson.

What Are Leaders Expected to Do?

While reviewing research on student collaboration, mathematical leaders need to seek examples of group-worthy problems that are currently available. These problems may be included in adopted textbooks or in curriculum guides. Students are highly social, and rudiments of collaboration can be effectively used to increase student engagement. However, true collaboration cannot be achieved without the use of challenging, rigorous, aligned, and appropriate group-worthy mathematical problems. Mathematics leaders must take the lead in providing these. Leaders should organize the search for necessary problem types, work with teachers to review items, and then work with teachers to test the items in classrooms.

Leaders also should help teachers balance lesson design and delivery. Students do not need to work in formal collaborative groups every class period nor have a group-worthy problem in every lesson. Overall balance and variety are important.

Leaders Ensure Proper Use of Group-Worthy Problems

Depending on a lesson's objectives and the length of the mathematics class, work on group-worthy problems may extend over several days. Teachers need to provide sufficient time for underlying concepts to be explored and developed. As illustrated in the previous examples, collaborative problem solving moves through three phases: setting the stage, exploration, and summary. Mathematics leaders should look for these three phases when reviewing teachers' lessons and consider these three phases when developing problems with teachers. Following are points to consider about each stage.

Setting the Stage

Teachers prepare students to undertake the assigned activities. Supporting concepts and skills are introduced along with desired learning objectives.

Teachers clearly explain the activities that students will be completing and establish general timelines for the tasks. This phase is a kind of balancing act for teachers. Sufficient information needs to be provided, but the task cannot be completed for students nor should expected results be detailed.

Exploration

Students work in collaborative teams, for the most part independently from teachers. Groups need to make decisions, carry out experiments, gather and organize data, and record outcomes. Collaborative teams provide a solution to the problem and organize answers into a presentation format. Teachers circulate throughout the room during group work, providing encouragement and support. Teachers may provide cues or ask prompting questions but may not complete the activity for students.

Summary

Students and teachers work together to draw out mathematical concepts revealed during exploration. This is a prime time for teachers to listen carefully to students in order to gauge their levels of understanding. Various solution approaches are compared, with emphasis again given to multiple representations of solutions.

During all three phases of this type of lesson, teachers should assess students' learning. Leaders also can play an important role in all three phases as another set of eyes when they visit classrooms. This does not mean that leaders sit in a corner of the classroom and critique. They should plan on actively engaging students and monitoring groups with teachers. Later, when teachers are reflecting on their experiences, leaders (even if they were not in the classroom during the lesson) can contribute to the discussion.

Resources That Leaders Can Use

Finding content-appropriate, group-worthy problems that align to state and district content standards can be challenging. Group-worthy problems are not—indeed, cannot be—an entire mathematics curriculum or the only instructional strategy used, and so these problems need to balance with other elements of the curriculum. Mathematics resources from the National Science Foundation often use a group-worthy problem format. There also are online resources that may be adapted. One useful website is the Charles A. Dana Center at the University of Texas at Austin (www.utdanacenter.org). Several mathematics textbook publishers also provide recommendations for group-worthy problems. Mathematics leaders must use care in evaluating problems to be used, regardless of their source. There are many mathematics activities available that are fun and engaging for students but do not convey the mathematics that students need.

Figure 5.1 is another example of a group-worthy problem that provides numerous opportunities for students to explore mathematics.

Figure 5.1 Group-Worthy Problem

How many circles are there in the picture below?

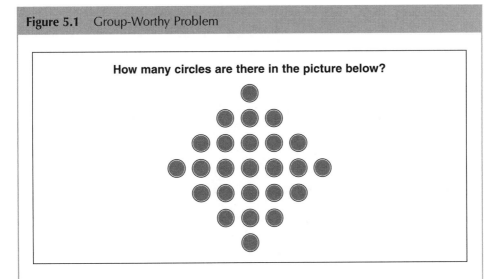

Setting the Stage

Hand out worksheets with the problem and several more arrays of circles on it. Also place a transparency on the overhead. Have students in groups determine the number of circles on the page (25). Most students will count.

Exploration

Have students work in their groups exploring how to find the answer of 25 in as many ways as possible. For each new way, have one student in each group capture the method by outlining circles on the page and have another student write an explanation of the method, along with an algebraic expression. Here is one method to consider: diagonally, notice $(4 \times 4) + (3 \times 3) = 16 + 9 = 25$.

Summarization

Have a member of each group write and/or show one method for finding the total of 25. Discuss the various methods. Then propose the following question: Is there a method that could best be used to solve any problem similar to this problem? For example, suppose we added another row of nine circles, does one of the methods help us solve this new problem? Does the one method illustrated above work? Lead students to a generalization for the problem:

$n^2 + (n - 1)^2 = T$, where n is the number of circles in an outside (exterior) diagonal and T is the total number of circles.

Collaboration is an effective classroom instructional strategy, but it should not be trivialized through overuse or inappropriate use. A range of mathematical tasks will be needed, and they all should be interesting and challenging.

INCORPORATING INSTRUCTIONAL STRATEGIES FOR ELL STUDENTS

Collaboration and group-worthy problems can serve another classroom need as well: providing supportive mathematical instruction for English language learners (ELL). Humans are social beings and structured classroom discussions of various kinds are vital to learning (National Resource Center, 2000). This is true for all students, but for ELL students, in particular, talking about mathematics is essential. Lessons that are built upon strategies that use principles of learning, that make thinking visible, and that address difficulties with language are more successful.

What Are Leaders Expected to Do?

Demographic shifts in population are changing U.S. public schools, but in many places instructional strategies have not made a corresponding shift. The need to use effective mathematics strategies is critical if the United States expects to compete in a global society (National Mathematics Advisory Panel, 2008). Strategies that increase learning for all students apply to ELL students as well, but there are additional strategies that can help teachers work effectively with this population.

Teachers of English language learners especially need to be well versed in a variety of instructional strategies that teach mathematical concepts and skills at appropriate grade levels and are suitable to overcome language barriers. In a study of how students learn conducted by the National Research Council (2005), the following fundamental learning principles were identified for teaching meaningful mathematics:

1. Students come to the classroom with preconceptions about how the world works. If their initial understanding is not engaged, they may fail to grasp the new concepts and information, or they may learn them for purposes of a test but revert to their preconceptions outside the classroom.

2. To develop competence in an area of inquiry, students must (a) have a deep foundation of factual knowledge, (b) understand facts and ideas in the context of a conceptual framework, and (c) organize knowledge in ways that facilitate retrieval and application.

3. A "metacognitive" approach to instruction can help students learn to take control of their own learning by defining learning goals and monitoring their progress in achieving them. (p. 1–2)

Two dynamics particularly affect ELL instruction. First, meaningful mathematics must be taught using strategies that reflect these three learning principles. Second, strategies must be used that also help students overcome language barriers. In many languages mathematical terms do not have the same meaning as in English, have a different cultural context, or may not readily translate. English phrases such as "increased/decreased by," "subtracted from," "divided into," or "more than" often cause problems for ELL students. Not only is vocabulary a stumbling block because some words have double and even triple meanings in either language, but there also is the issue of process. Unlike mathematics curricula in the United States, with their focus on process standards (emphasizing problem solving), mathematics programs in other cultures often dwell on getting correct answers at the expense of fully understanding the mathematics involved. Thus, English language learners may have trouble explaining or justifying the mathematics they used to solve problems because the problem-solving processes they were taught in their native country or their own thought processes may be entirely different from what is commonly understood in this country.

Leaders Ensure Use of Effective Strategies for ELL Students

Four points merit discussion. First, mathematics leaders should be prepared to share with teachers the difficulties that English language learners face when they first study mathematics as it is taught in American schools. A cursory Internet search will provide a long list of available resources for ELL students, many specific to cultural backgrounds. Many instructional materials from major publishers also are now sensitive to cultural differences and provide resources. Glossaries and dictionaries are usually available to help teachers cope with basic word translations.

Mathematics curricula in other countries—especially developing nations—may be computation oriented, without geometry or other topics familiar in American schools. Some they/we comparisons include:

- Rote learning rather than conceptual understanding as a focus,
- Metric measurements rather than U.S. standard measurements,
- Unfamiliar number formations used in particular by various non-Western cultures,
- Unfamiliar verbal problem-solving techniques,

- Unfamiliar use of punctuation symbols, and
- Hands-on activities using unfamiliar cultural norms.

Teachers need to be cognizant of these differences and plan lessons for ELL students accordingly.

Second, mathematics leaders, if possible in conjunction with ELL specialists, should be able to provide information to teachers that will aid in determining ELL students' levels of English proficiency as related to mathematics. This background information will help leaders and teachers set realistic expectations for ELL students.

Third, mathematics leaders should provide teachers with learning strategies that are social in approach. Interaction and communication are important to ELL students' learning. Oxford (1990) classifies social communication strategies according to three activities in which students engage:

- Asking questions.
  1. Asking for clarification or verification.
  2. Asking for correction.
- Cooperating with others.
  1. Cooperating with peers.
  2. Cooperating with proficient users of the new language.
- Empathizing with others.
  1. Developing cultural understanding.
  2. Becoming aware of others' thoughts and feelings. (p. 18–21)

Fourth, mathematics leaders need to share specific strategies that have been found to be effective in working with English language learners, strategies that in many cases work with all students. The ideal instructional sequence and selection of strategies will be one that teaches students content to master in the shortest reasonable time. To approach this goal, individual strategies and combinations of strategies must be carefully selected. Some strategies will take additional up-front time, while others will require extra exploration or practice time for ELL students. Instructional balance will be required. Teachers who use a single dominant strategy, no matter how effective it is or might be at times, will not find it to be optimally effective all the time. By the same token, teachers cannot include every possible strategy in every lesson. Teachers need to apply the right cluster of strategies for the right situation.

Resources That Leaders Can Use

Consistent with findings such as those from various National Research Council studies, strategies that engage students, work within a context, and encourage students to self-monitor their thinking should be used regularly. An example of such a strategy can be seen in the random-digits activity shown in Figure 5.2.

Clustering effective strategies is also important. Global strategies, described previously, help teachers structure strategy clusters that incorporate more specific strategies, such as the one in Figure 5.2. Strategy clusters can be structured for teachers to use at specific times, for example, when launching an instructional unit or teaching a lesson that students usually find difficult. Clusters also can be constructed for certain purposes, such as to assist in overcoming language barriers or for scaffolding key concepts. An important approach for academic success is combining instructional strategies that address the needs of the students—and, of course, needs vary from time to time.

The two global strategies discussed earlier (collaboration and group-worthy problems) are highly recommended and provide multiple opportunities to incorporate additional strategies, but they do not have to be in place for teachers to draw on specific strategies that still can be effective. Teachers may not have access to group-worthy problems that meet the learning needs of ELL students, or they simply may not yet be comfortable

---

Figure 5.2   Random Digits

One activity that has worked exceptionally well with ELL teachers and students, in fact with all students, deals with random digits. The directions are simple: Use any operation (addition, subtraction, multiplication, or division), an equal sign, and parentheses if needed, to create a correct number sentence. The number sentences can be horizontal or vertical. Two or more digits can be used to make a number. Shown below is a part of the random digit sheet used for the activity.

6	0	5	2	4	9	3	8	1	6	3	7	0	5	9	2	4	7	1	8
1	8	1	8	0	6	0	2	5	9	1	4	9	1	8	6	9	0	3	0
5	0	9	4	7	2	9	4	8	0	6	3	5	7	1	4	1	8	7	6
2	7	1	6	5	3	2	0	2	4	8	1	2	6	9	7	3	5	1	4

with collaborative grouping. Specific strategies still must be aligned with the principles of learning identified by the National Research Council.

Effective teaching uses techniques that build on student understandings and confront misconceptions (National Research Council, 2000). This is why it is so fundamental to use instructional strategies that make students' thinking visible to teachers and students alike. Instructional techniques that assist ELL students in achieving mathematics mastery also help students who are native English speakers, though the converse is not necessarily true. For ELL students, teachers should be attuned to using strategies that increase student dialogue and pictorially represent student thinking. By verbalizing, creating concept maps, and producing diagrams, ELL students can bring to a concrete, visible level their thoughts and understandings. Other elements of instructional strategies that are effective with ELL students include repetition of important concepts and vocabulary, concrete examples, and modeling thought processes aloud. Within the "safe" environments of student pairs or teams and a trusting classroom, the following strategies can be used to encourage students to think about, to rethink, and, if necessary, to reconceptualize their mathematical understandings.

Partner or Peer Tutoring

As described by Wagner (2005), partner or peer tutoring is an instructional strategy that increases student dialogue but allows teachers to maintain classroom control. Students check their understanding of a mathematical concept or skill, working with a partner. This allows mistakes or errors to be caught early so that misunderstandings can be corrected before they get in the way of new learning. Pair reading, reading aloud, and summarizing information can be effectively carried out in partner teams. Partner or peer tutoring can be used in conjunction with any of the other specific strategies described below.

Vocabulary Building

Mathematics content is difficult to read, often because of its specialized vocabulary. Mathematical vocabulary can be classified into four categories, according to Monroe and Panchyshyn (1989):

1. Technical—mathematical words that have only meaning which is specific to mathematics

2. Subtechnical—words that vary in meaning from one content area to another

3. General—words in everyday language

4. Symbolic—common math symbols and corresponding expressions

Mathematics leaders and teachers should discuss the vocabulary needs for particular areas of the curriculum, looking for ways to clarify language for all students but especially for English language learners.

Organizing Concepts

Models, pictorial representations, graphic organizers, or flow charts that show whole-to-part can help students make associations among content elements (Marzano, 2001). Graphic organizers or concept maps help students identify critical elements and terms and the relationships between them. One such organizer is shown in Figure 5.3, called a KWLH Chart. K represents what students *know;* W what they *want* to learn, L what they have *learned,* and H *how* they can learn more. Students complete each column of the table as they learn about various mathematical concepts.

Another organizer is called a Series of Events Chain. Each piece of information is related to the next piece of information in some way. Two examples are provided in Figure 5.4.

According to Starnes (2006), displays, diagrams, and charts simplify information and allow students to see patterns. Before starting an instructional unit teachers should provide students with an overview using pictures, charts, or diagrams or allow students to construct organizers around their current knowledge in order to set a firm foundation of prior knowledge on which to build new understandings (Jensen, 1998).

Technology Use

For many English language learners, using calculators or computers will be a new experience. Calculators allow students to test hypotheses, to see patterns, and to reinforce mathematical learning without completing long, sometimes complex computations. Computer programs can facilitate the use of graphic images for many mathematical topics. Mathematics leaders and staff need to have up-to-date skills in the use of various, commonly available technologies.

Scaffolding

Scaffolding reminds students of important prerequisite concepts and skills prior to immersion into new material. Structuring activities around these skills prior to introducing new material is well worth teachers' time.

Figure 5.3 KWLH Chart

What We Know	What We Want to Learn	What We Learned	How Can We Learn More

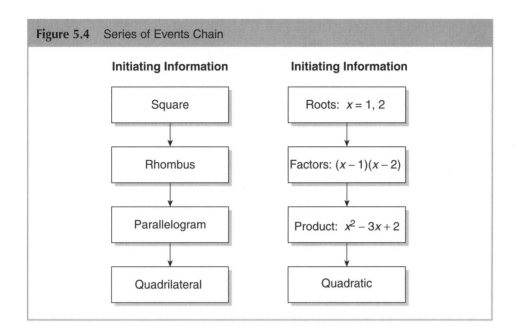

Figure 5.4   Series of Events Chain

Initiating Information	Initiating Information
Square	Roots: $x = 1, 2$
Rhombus	Factors: $(x - 1)(x - 2)$
Parallelogram	Product: $x^2 - 3x + 2$
Quadrilateral	Quadratic

Questions to consider include: How can content be made comprehensible for learners? How can new content be linked to students' prior knowledge? What teaching aids should be prepared or purchased before teaching a lesson?

Transfer

Positive and negative transfer are not instructional strategies per se, but they greatly influence the effectiveness of some strategies and aid in the selection of others. Transfer is a learning phenomenon that is critical for teachers to understand. Students and adults form connective networks to understand and retrieve information. They seek attributes that seem to make sense and are based on their current level of understanding and then file the new information accordingly. As an example of negative transfer, students routinely confuse the terms and mathematical calculations for mean, median, and mode. The words all start with the letter *m* and usually are taught in the same unit. They are statistical measures calculated using the same set of numbers. Without emphasis over time and ample opportunities for students to discuss how the measures are similar and different, the concepts will regularly be confused (National Research Council, 2000).

Teachers need to stress similarities and differences to help students distinguish critical attributes. Identifying similarities and differences helps students make conscious associations by comparing important characteristics and can be used by teachers at any time (Marzano, 2001).

MATCHING MATERIALS TO DESIRED INSTRUCTIONAL STRATEGIES

Mathematics leaders faced with growing demands for academic improvement must find ways to help teachers more fully engage students in the learning process. Lessons built on strategies that use the researched-based instructional ideas presented in this book will be successful. And materials chosen or designed to support effective strategies will be easiest for teachers to implement fully and therefore will likely achieve the best learning results.

What Are Leaders Expected to Do?

The phrase "instructional materials" is broad. Depending on the state or district, it can refer to textbooks, tests or other assessment instruments, technology-based materials, and other instructional materials, including related or optional manipulatives. Most states provide for textbook adoption in some form, either by local districts or at the state level, often with the requirement that the textbook be aligned to state and national standards. Mathematics leaders are expected to have current knowledge about available instructional materials and should be able to provide information to staff or to structure opportunities for staff to learn about current or forthcoming materials.

Leaders Ensure That Materials Match Instructional Strategies

When districts are permitted to adopt materials locally, mathematics leaders must be involved in making adoption decisions. They will need to consider certain questions: Is a particular material approved by the state? Does it align with the local curriculum plan? Leaders help teachers understand alignment issues with individual textbooks, series, and other instructional materials.

Resources That Leaders Can Use

Many states offer instructional materials, evaluation criteria, and scoring rubrics for districts and schools to use in making selections. Common threads in the criteria are evident. As an example, California (California Department of Education, 2007, p. 4) offers the following categories:

California Evaluation Criteria

The criteria for the evaluation of mathematics instructional resources for kindergarten through Grade 8 are divided into five categories:

1. Mathematics content/alignment with the standards

2. Program organization

3. Assessment

4. Universal access

5. Instructional planning and support

Mathematics leaders should be current in their knowledge of categories and criteria to assist districts, schools, and departments in decisions that need to be made. In addition, states often provide criteria that focus on the multicultural aspects of instructional materials.

Mathematics leaders must have current knowledge of various criteria that can assist districts, schools, and departments in making decisions about potential materials. Appropriate questions include:

- Is the content accurate?
- Does the material cover process skills (problem solving, communication, reasoning and proof, connections, representation)?
- Is the material age appropriate?
- Is the material pedagogically sound? Does it cover a wide range of instructional strategies?

Other criteria may focus on the physical characteristics of materials, including:

- Are the materials durable?
- Are they readable as intended (print size, highlighting)?
- Are graphs, tables, and pictures appropriate? Are they labeled correctly?
- Do they contain guide sections (table of contents, glossary, index)?
- Are related teacher materials, student materials, and parent materials available?
- Does the presentation of the content reflect the needs of diverse populations?

Supplementary materials, such as manipulatives and technology, require different criteria, including:

- Are manipulatives supplied?
- Can the manipulatives be purchased economically?
- Is the required or included technology user friendly?
- Are manuals for manipulatives and technology easy to understand by teachers and students?

- Do the manipulatives and technology enhance student learning?
- Do they add depth to the learning experience?

Finally, for core textbooks or series, mathematics leaders must be prepared to guide a team in evaluating assessment options by asking the following questions:

- Are various assessment options provided?
- Do the assessments match local objectives?
- Are scoring tools and rubrics readily available?

USING DATA TO INFORM PRACTICE 1: ANALYZING STUDENT WORK

Mathematics leaders must work to ensure that teachers use data to analyze the effectiveness of strategies matched to content. This takes two main forms: analyzing student work and analyzing student assessment results. The first is discussed in this section; the second in the next section. Teachers need to be able to use both forms of analysis to understand whether strategies are effective and how to modify teaching practices as necessary. As Williams (1996) points out, there is a strong relationship between assessment, instruction, and achievement.

What Are Leaders Expected to Do?

Teachers routinely use various forms of informal assessment during instruction, for example, by carefully observing and listening to students as they study or engage in group activities. Teachers need to reflect on student learning, and analyzing student work is one of the informal assessment strategies that can serve this purpose. Mathematics leaders can play an important role in helping teachers understand and use informal assessment strategies. For example, leaders can engage teachers in structured conversations concerning misunderstandings and misconceptions that students have about content. Questions might include: What common errors do students make? What prerequisite knowledge or skills do students often lack? What should teachers look for during a lesson? What types of questions should teachers ask to ensure students' understanding? What written assignments should be generated? Which assignments are for a grade, and how will they be graded? Finally, what informal work do students produce as evidence of learning?

Leaders Help Teachers Analyze Student Work

Teachers do not have training or time to create curricula *as* they teach. The foundation is present in curriculum documents, and what teachers must do is adjust for the individual needs of students or classes of students. Leaders can help teachers make these adjustments while remaining true to the curriculum objectives. Leaders should assist in clarifying expectations for student work prior to a lesson, frequently attending parts of a lesson during instruction to observe and occasionally offering advice, and helping teachers reflect on lesson outcomes by collaborating to review student work.

When reviewing and analyzing student work with teachers, looking at each and every paper is not necessary or even desirable. In fact, students' names can be removed because the work should not receive a grade, and previous work by individual students is not a factor. Leaders help teachers analyze the work to determine whether learning goals are being met and to pinpoint strengths and weaknesses in assigned activities.

One approach is to center a professional conversation on a sample of student work. Teachers begin by identifying the sample—for instance, several representative papers—that they believe best exemplifies the desired outcomes of a particular assignment or task. Leaders conduct a conversation to identify criteria. What makes this sample exemplary? What were students able to do, show, or explain that indicates they understood the learning objectives and grasped the target concepts?

Next, teachers randomly select other papers from the same assignment to analyze. Do these papers match the exemplary sample, or are they lacking in some of the criteria? If they do not measure up in some way, what did students miss? How great is the gap between these papers and the exemplary ones?

This process continues until teachers believe that they have a good understanding of the strengths and weaknesses exhibited by their students. Based on this information, they can plan the next lesson or unit. By organizing the future lesson around students' demonstrated strengths and an understanding of students' weaknesses, teachers can incorporate targeted strategies, such as scaffolding, embedding practice, and grouping, that will lead students to greater success.

Resources That Leaders Can Use

A top priority for leaders is to assist teachers in keeping student tasks and learning objectives closely aligned to identified state and local standards. Copies of standards need to be readily available. Analysis of student work must be directly linked to performance outcomes derived from these standards.

Even though a district may sanction certain instructional materials, such approval does not ensure alignment of all elements to identified standards. Leaders will need to work with teachers to make appropriate adjustments in some cases.

Below are examples illustrating a couple of ways that teachers can go about using assignments in which analysis is implicit in the form of the assignment.

EXAMPLES OF INFORMAL ASSESSMENT

Example 1

Teachers may have students complete an open-ended question such as:

John and Mary both have change in their pocket. Both have more than 50 cents but less than $1.00. Mary has 15 cents more than John. How much money do you think each student has in his or her pocket and why do you think this?

Students could draw coins or write a description, or both. Teachers may read over the work, or interview students.

Example 2

Teachers could also have students independently write out the answer to a question related to the group activity in which they have been working, such as:

Name two pairs of equivalent fractions. Explain why they are equivalent. Draw a picture to demonstrate.

Leaders need to help teachers keep in mind that analyzing student work has a different purpose from analyzing student assessments. It is an informal process that can be embedded in a lesson and used in conjunction with formal assessments to inform instruction. Informal assessments that result from analyzing student work are designed to answer questions such as:

- Does the class understand concepts from the lesson?
- Are several students making specific errors?
- Do I need to spend more time on the topic, or can I move on?

Use of an informal assessment technique of analyzing student work also helps teachers know when to employ more formal assessments.

USING DATA TO INFORM PRACTICE 2: ANALYZING STUDENT ASSESSMENTS

Teachers and leaders in our experience seem to be more comfortable with analyzing assessments than with analyzing student work. Teachers regularly give formal assessments in the form of tests, and districts in some fashion generally require tests. Many tests result in grades for individual students and may be used to evaluate student learning in general. Leaders must recognize that this form of testing is far removed from giving and analyzing assessments in order to inform practice. According to the National Research Council (2000), "The roles of assessment must be expanded beyond the traditional concept of testing. The use of frequent formative assessment helps make student's thinking visible to themselves, their peers, and their teacher" (p. 19).

What Are Leaders Expected to Do?

Leaders need to help teachers understand differences between testing for a grade and assessing for student understanding. Testing for a grade does not provide adequate analysis, even if students correct their mistakes. Tests are usually given, graded, recorded, and returned to students. In assessing for understanding, teachers try to understand what students know and what they can do so that future lessons can be shaped accordingly. Such assessments may take many forms, for example, multiple-choice or essay questions. Teachers need students to display and clarify their knowledge and thinking in reference to particular objectives. Consequently, creating and analyzing assessments usually requires more time and effort than a teacher can manage alone. Teachers also may be limited in their access to student assessments from other teachers, which can provide valuable insights.

Leaders must ensure that a wide variety of assessment types are used and set clear expectations for each type. Leaders may need to provide teachers with appropriate assessments or samples. They then must work to be certain that the assessments are administered consistently throughout the district, using an appropriate timeline and common guidelines. Next, leaders must guide appropriate analysis and see that data are distributed and shared in compliance with district policies and guidelines. Finally, leaders need to help teachers apply what they have learned from the data.

Leaders Help Teachers Analyze Student Assessments

Leaders need to start with the current level of teachers' understanding. Mathematics teachers, accustomed to giving weekly tests that are easily graded, may not immediately embrace assessments that are designed to make student thinking visible and that require in-depth analysis through conversations with colleagues or mathematics leaders.

Leaders will need to help create assessments, identify criteria for mastery, engage in collegial conversations concerning the assessments, and lead conversations about using data to inform practice. Leaders must help teachers see links between assessment, instructional strategies, and student learning.

At first, leaders probably should simply encourage in-depth analysis of data generated from the current testing process. By analyzing data in more depth than teachers may be used to, leaders can discuss with teachers questions such as:

- What do you think was done to get students to answer these questions correctly?
- What is your general sense of what students know and do not know?
- Why do you suppose so many students picked answer X for this problem?
- What is it about this distracter that confused students?
- If you could do one thing again before giving this test, what would it be?
- Do you see any patterns forming among students who didn't do well compared to those who did do well?

As leaders engage them in these conversations, teachers will begin to appreciate the value of analyzing data. A natural outcome is to want more types of data. This should open the door for discussions about open-ended assessments that require students to show their work and to justify their reasoning, thus providing more information for teachers to consider.

On a related note, leaders also may need to help formulate grading rubrics that ensure equity in the treatment of graded assignments. Creating and following grading guidelines requires practice, and leaders can help teachers hone their skills in this area.

Resources That Leaders Can Use

Marzano (2003) states, "The message is clear. Unless a school employs assessments that are specific to the curriculum actually taught, it cannot accurately determine how well its students are learning" (p. 38). If he is correct, then leaders must carefully match curriculum content and assessment. Leaders cannot assume that purchased assessments, or even locally written ones, are aligned. However, leaders will want to start with assessments already developed and on hand. They should review such assessments by asking several questions:

- Are the essential objectives adequately tested?
- Is the test an adequate demonstration of mastery of the concepts?
- Does the test use a variety of formats?
- In addition to the test results, what other data would be helpful?
- Which objectives should be assessed using an open-ended format?
- What tasks might students be asked to do that would indicate strong conceptual understanding?

For examples of assessment items a good resource is the Charles A. Dana Center at the University of Texas at Austin (www.utdanacenter.org). Items online are free to download. As previously noted, most states also make available items or sample items from their assessments. An example of such an assessment from the Charles A. Dana Center website, related to Texas content standards, is shown below.

EXAMPLE OF ASSESSMENT ITEM

Fourth-Grade Texas Essential Knowledge and Skills (TEKS)

Standards

(4.6) Patterns, relationships, and algebraic thinking. The student uses patterns in multiplication and division.

(4.6.a) Patterns, relationships, and algebraic thinking. The student uses patterns in multiplication and division. The student is expected to use patterns and relationships to develop strategies to remember basic multiplication and division facts (such as the patterns in related multiplication and division number sequences (fact families) such as $9 \times 9 = 81$ and $81 \div 9 = 9$).

Clarifying Activity With Assessment Connections

On grid paper, students form a rectangular model for a multiplication problem such as 6×12, 7×12, or 8×12. They cover the grid paper with base-ten blocks and are guided into recognizing the pattern of the distributive property of multiplication over addition, for example, $7 \times 12 = 7 \times (10 + 2) = (7 \times 10) + (7 \times 2) = 70 + 14 = 84$.

Students use this pattern to check 9×12. Students then use grid paper (with markers now) to model $7 \times 6 = (5 + 2) \times 6$, and $3 \times 9 = 3 \times (10 - 1) = (3 \times 10) - 3$. The students extend the pattern to break down a "hard-to-remember" multiplication fact into two more easily remembered multiplication facts.

(Continued)

(Continued)

Each student develops a personal list of "tough" facts to remember and shows ways the facts can be broken down to make them easier to remember.

Assessment Connections

Questioning

Open with . . .

Tell me about your hard-to-remember multiplication facts and how you might use this pattern to remember them.

Probe further with . . .

- What are some multiplication facts that you don't always recall?
- How can you break this down into facts you do remember?
- How did we break down 7 x 6? Can you extend this approach to break down your hard-to-remember fact? How?
- How did you decide how to break it down? Did you draw a picture? Did you use paper and pencil? Did you do this in your head?
- Are there other ways you could break this down? How?

Listen for . . .

- Can the student explain the strategy used to break down (partition) hard-to-remember facts?
- Does the student check for the reasonableness of the solution?

Look for . . .

- Does the student notice the pattern of the distributive property of multiplication over addition (subtraction)? (Note: Students will not identify with terminology such as distributive property.)
- Can the student apply the pattern of the distributive property of multiplication over addition (subtraction)?
- Can the student use the pattern of the distribution of multiplication over addition (subtraction) to create strategies that can help figure out hard-to-remember multiplication facts?
- Can the student break down hard-to-remember multiplication facts into two multiplication facts that can be used to find the product of the hard-to-remember one?
- Does the student use mental arithmetic, paper and pencil, or a rectangular model to break down the hard-to-remember facts?
- Does the student apply this method to help remember facts on other occasions?
- Is the student able to self-correct?

6

Providing Timely and Targeted Feedback

Many of the preceding chapters have dealt with engaging teachers in the process of change to improve students' learning and increase achievement, particularly with an eye toward closing the achievement gap. The developmental stage of providing timely, targeted feedback shifts the role of mathematics leaders toward empowering teachers. Engagement is about teachers *doing* certain things; empowerment is about *believing*. Feedback appropriately collected and used serves as a tipping point for change. Supportive, specific feedback accelerates the teaching/learning process and increases student achievement (Reeves, 2004). The data we discuss in this chapter are to be used in conjunction with information from classroom visits.

Empowerment brings about a sense of efficacy for teachers on two points. First, teachers believe that all students can learn mathematics and, second, they believe that they can successfully teach them. These beliefs are crucial because, as we noted in earlier chapters, teachers have the greatest effect on student learning and feedback is the strongest educational tool that teachers can use to structure practice and thereby improve student outcomes (Stronge, 2007; Marzano, Walters, & McNulty, 2005).

While feedback is critical for successful improvement, it also can be a double-edged sword. When used correctly, it is positive and motivating; when misused, it is punitive, misleading, and disheartening. Without care in types and degrees of feedback, teachers can receive mixed messages with dire consequences. As Reeves (2004) points out:

> These teachers likely doubt the other feedback that they receive, ultimately regarding themselves as personal and professional failures. Once they give up hope, perception becomes reality, as their formerly heroic efforts give way to passivity. Their relentless optimism is overtaken by a sense of helplessness, with the former "You can do it!" replaced by "Nothing I do will make a difference." (p. 57)

Feedback at benchmark and classroom-visit levels uses whole-school improvement data and does not target individual teachers. Thus, mathematics leaders should seek supporting data about program implementation and students' learning of mathematics. They will need to pay attention to effective implementation, and that can be far more challenging than one might expect.

Mathematics leaders will need evidence to change instructional beliefs. Dissonance must be created regarding beliefs on which current teaching is based. Deeply engrained biases, such as "only some students can learn mathematics," must be challenged in order to be changed. The chances that change will be made without adequate feedback are slim. And even when progress is made, without feedback no one can say for certain what actions created the improvement. Feedback is essential to sustain both daily improvement efforts and long-term initiatives.

USING PERTINENT DATA

According to Fenwick English (2000), "The minute that curriculum becomes focused on and connected to, as well as aligned with tests, the influence of socioeconomic level on test performance declines" (p. 6). For these connections to be made, monitoring and feedback are essential. "Regular monitoring, followed by adjustments, is the only way to expect success" (Schmoker, 1999, p. 5). A first step for leaders will be gathering accurate, meaningful data that support instructional changes by teachers and that lead to increased learning by students. Data that are collected, but not provided as appropriate feedback, are useless. To be useful, feedback data must be relevant and specific.

What Are Leaders Expected to Do?

Feedback takes two basic forms: evaluative and supportive. These two forms reinforce our earlier discussions concerning management and leadership and the double-edged sword of feedback. Mathematics leaders will be expected to understand differences between evaluative and supportive data and to work closely with principals to keep these two forms of data separate. Principals traditionally evaluate; therefore, principals are the educators we will primarily discuss in relation to evaluative data. Mathematics leaders, who routinely work with principals, should avoid collecting or using evaluative data on teachers unless they are specifically assigned such duties.

Evaluative and supportive feedback merit further discussion to clarify the nature of each. Evaluative data collection and feedback are limited to line-authority personnel, such as principals and superintendents. Principals who want to change classroom practices need to shift between roles of manager and instructional leader. Part of this shift is understanding the difference between evaluative feedback and supportive feedback. Evaluation data are used to examine something in order to judge its value, quality, or importance. Administrators usually are required to conduct some form of teacher evaluation based on established criteria. Data collection normally is fairly standardized, and principals are trained in proper personnel evaluation methods in order to ensure equality and accuracy. However, evaluation rarely changes behavior in a meaningful way. Evaluations and monitoring for evaluations are management tasks used to measure compliance to rules and to answer the question: Does the mathematics teacher exhibit appropriate professional characteristics? The designated criteria used to make evaluative judgments are broader than the criteria used to gather supportive data.

Supportive data collection examines trends and patterns of instruction and learning exhibited by groups rather than individuals. Feedback conversations about such data are concerned with specific instructional strategies and resulting student learning. Supportive monitoring and feedback are leadership tasks and answer the question: Is the mathematics department accurately implementing the adopted curriculum and using recommended instructional strategies? Schmoker (1999) suggests that school success requires adoption of an instructionally effective and standards-based mathematics program, plus a high degree of program implementation with fidelity. Monitoring the degree of implementation and providing supportive feedback to teachers produce student achievement results.

Unlike evaluative data, supportive data are specific to implementation of the mathematics program. Data are collected on attributes determined to be crucial for learning, such as student grouping, lesson objectives, and use of manipulatives.

Supportive data collection and feedback are not limited to specific job designations. Any staff member may participate as long as confidentiality rules are followed. However, evaluative data and supportive data should never be mixed. Teachers who are working hard to implement an engaging mathematics activity using a grouping approach in an exploratory setting, for example, must not be "written up" (in other words, given a negative evaluation) for having paper on the floor.

In many cases, mathematics leaders are communication links with administrators and teachers, with information flowing both ways. Occasional meetings need to occur in which principals, mathematics leaders, and teachers discuss roles, responsibilities, communications, improvement plans, and so on. Principals may see mathematics leaders as allies and extra hands in collecting evaluative data or pinpointing certain teachers' weaknesses. Therefore, ground rules are useful to delineate mathematics leaders' roles in focusing on collecting and using supportive, rather than evaluative, data.

Mathematics leaders may be under district restrictions with regard to some aspects of data availability and control, such as how data may be collected, when and by whom, and how they are reported. Leaders should focus solely on supportive data, and with a definite purpose in mind they can better determine what data are needed and how the data can best be reported. Starting small to ensure that data are collected and returned in a timely manner usually is advisable.

Information from classroom visits and benchmark data can be used to work with teachers to connect strategies to learning results. Teacher empowerment develops through studying and reflecting on such connections (Short & Greer, 2002). Data aid in showing the effect these strategies have on students' involvement and engagement in mathematics activities.

Leaders Help Teachers Use Pertinent Data

Mathematics leaders should regularly discuss data with principals and teachers. Reports to principals usually will be about general trends. Leaders also may provide information that emphasizes strategies on including such trends in classrooms. Student data will show progress (or its absence) over time. Principals will want information about progress but also about difficulties and where attention is needed. They need to hear about interventions and about which students should be given special assistance. For teachers, the data will best be reported by classroom and in comparison to other sections of the same course.

Resources That Leaders Can Use

Data should be charted over time to demonstrate progress, verify efforts, and identify both positive and negative results. Although leaders need to be realistic and honest, their overall purpose is to encourage continued efforts at change and improvement. Various levels of data are needed to correspond to the levels of "need to know"—central office administration, principals, teachers, and mathematics leaders themselves. Reports may reflect the immediate concerns and interests of each level or a longer-term perspective. The following breakdowns may be useful:

For central office administrators

Classroom-visit data

- Districtwide by school over time
- Shifts in strategies organized by elementary, middle, and high schools
- Benchmark assessment data
- Districtwide percent passing by grade level
- Progress shown over time
- Significant populations reported by grade level
- School ranking by elementary, middle, and high schools

For principals

Classroom-visit data

- Schoolwide by grade level or course
- Shifts in strategy use over time

Benchmark assessment data

- School-level student passing percentage by teacher
- Comparisons with similar schools
- Significant or identified populations by percent passing by course
- Progress over time by course

For teachers

Classroom-visit data

- Schoolwide by grade level or course
- Shifts in strategies by course over time

Benchmark assessment data

- Student scores by class percent passing
- Item analysis by class
- Significant populations by percentage passing
- Individual student scores by item

This list should be viewed only as a starting point for mathematics leaders to think about differentiated data and reports for various audiences. Each school and district will have specific information needs.

TARGETED INFORMATION

Complementing the preceding point, mathematics leaders should understand that information needs to be targeted for populations and purposes. Data must be specific in order to have the desired impact on efficacy and empowerment (Stronge, 2007). The critical point here is that leaders must emphasize that teachers' actions result in students' actions that either block or facilitate learning and academic achievement.

What Are Leaders Expected to Do?

Data must meet teachers' needs as individuals and within professional groups. Teachers have a vast array of skills, experiences, and talents; therefore, they also have diverse needs when it comes to understanding and implementing improvement initiatives. Mathematics leaders rarely have the luxury of being able to meet with every teacher individually, and so they must build collegial working environments in which they and teachers can share expertise (Short & Greer, 2002). Particularly when teachers demonstrate specific expertise, it falls to leaders to ensure that they can share that expertise with their colleagues.

Leaders Help Teachers Use Targeted Information

Mathematics leaders control the amount of data that will be collected, analyzed, and reported. Using data is a skill that evolves over time. Trying to institute multiple change initiatives and collect data on each one can be overwhelming and thus is usually counterproductive (Marzano, Walters, & McNulty, 2005). Leaders also should be cautious about overwhelming teachers with too many change expectations, which can send a message that none of the current practices are correct and leave teachers feeling confused, frustrated, and defeated before they even begin.

Mathematics leaders need to work closely with teachers and carefully review research to determine initiatives and strategies that seem likely to have the greatest effect on student learning. Teachers will need to try new instructional techniques, and leaders must support these efforts. Change takes time, and not every attempt will be successful. Teachers will need targeted information and specific feedback to try new approaches and then assess their effect.

Teachers also will need help providing information to students that goes beyond traditional grades. Students need to understand the degree to which they have demonstrated learning (Stronge, 2007). Students who earn high grades should be proud of their achievement. But students who do not score high still need to be acknowledged for the learning they were able to demonstrate and encouraged to increase their level of learning. Teachers too often are quick to undervalue the learning achieved by students scoring at, say, the 65-percent level. However, such students have demonstrated a fair amount of understanding of material, and that learning can provide the steppingstones to greater achievement. After all, the difference between "pass" and "fail" may be only one or two questions. Marzano and his colleagues (2005) comment, "When students perceive that they have progressed in the acquisition of knowledge or skill, they tend to increase their level of effort and engagement regardless of their relative standing compared with other students" (p. 96).

Students learn in various ways and at their own pace (National Research Council, 2000). Effective intervention when learning difficulties arise should not automatically trigger reteaching, especially when reteaching means merely repeating the same lesson. Leaders must assist teachers in identifying strategies targeted to individual students' learning needs. Teachers also must recognize that intervention efforts outside the mathematics classroom (through special classes or tutoring) are most effective when directly related to the content that the students are learning in the classroom.

Some teachers will be eager, early adopters, while others will take a wait-and-see approach or may actively resist change. Therefore, mathematics leaders also must target their efforts to get teachers on board with the improvement initiative to the teachers' individual needs and perspectives. Early adopters and cautious adopters will likely be the two groups that can most easily be brought into the improvement effort. The resisters will be harder to entice, but success in the other groups will have a spillover effect to encourage them. Leadership that targets information that specifically helps resisters become adopters can then enhance the spillover effect.

Resources That Leaders Can Use

Mathematics leaders and teachers need to share a vision of what daily mathematics instruction should look like and what implementation of the adopted curriculum means (Short & Greer, 2002). Certain instructional strategies will be targeted, or emphasized, during professional development sessions. For example, we have already discussed the classroom-visit tallies. Let us say that "students are demonstrating understanding" was noted infrequently, perhaps twice in seven visits. Leaders could target this factor and guide teachers to consider related actions from the tallies that might enhance or improve this factor. This might lead teachers to focus on getting students to

- work collaboratively in small groups,
- share or explain their thinking, and
- investigate complementary mathematical concepts.

At the same time, if a factor is noted fairly frequently, perhaps during five of seven classroom visits, then teachers might be urged to discuss the quality of the actions that produced this result and ponder whether a disconnect might exist between the frequently and seldomly observed factors and why.

Teachers also should relate this analysis to results from benchmark assessments and later to their analysis of student work. For example, when teachers used grouping strategies, did the students appear to be more involved in solving challenging problems? Perhaps the tallied actions seemed to allow students to respond correctly to assessment items such as the following:

Elementary school

Mary, Sam, Susan, and Bob ordered one medium pizza each. After eating all they wanted, they each took their remaining pizza home. Mary ate 3/8 of her pizza, Sam ate 1/4 of his pizza, Susan ate 3/4 of her pizza, and Bob ate 1/2 of his pizza. Who took the most pizza home?

A. Mary   B. Sam   C. Susan   D. Bob

Middle school

Sally's living room needs new flooring. She has 36 square yards of carpeting but wants to put down wood tiling. How many square feet of wood tiling does she need?

A. 36
square feet

B. 72
square feet

C. 144
square feet

D. 324
square feet

High school

Maria wants a new CD player. She went online and found the following prices for players in stores near her home: $80.00, $95.00, $60.00, $90.00, and $85.00. She wants to tell her parents the average price of a new CD player. What price would she say?

A. $45.00

B. $410.00

C. $ 85.00

D. $82.00

On the other hand, concern was raised because students failed to respond correctly to items such as the following:

Elementary school

Tony was sent to the store to buy hamburger for a casserole. He was told to buy seven-tenths of a pound. Which is the correct label he should select?

A. 7.10
pounds

B. 1.7
pounds

C. 0.7
pound

D. 0.17
pound

Middle school

Julia's new family car gets about 27 miles per gallon of gas. The family can travel 408 miles before running out of gas. What is the greatest number of gallons of gas the family car can hold?

A. 13
gallons

B. 15
gallons

C. 24
gallons

D. 27
gallons

High school

At W.C. Smith High School there are 2 athletes out of every 5 students. What percent of the students are not athletes?

A. 40%

B. 60%

C. 20%

D. 50%

With these hypothetical problems there are no correct answers for why students may have responded to some correctly and to others incorrectly. However, in real classrooms teachers need to be able to understand what is happening with students during assessments that caused them to select alternate choices. On the surface, teachers may not be able to explain the differences or can only hypothesize. Explanations are especially difficult for assessments that are multiple-choice with no student work attached. Without an understanding of students' thinking, intervention strategies often are ineffective. Teachers may decide, perhaps without good reason, to reteach an entire concept based on a few items for which students

- made a common calculation error,
- jumped to a solution because of a similar practice item,
- worked correctly but misread the question,
- ran out of time and took a guess, or
- did not understand a question or vocabulary.

If teachers do not listen—or do not understand how to listen—to students, then they may not realize how confusing a problem is or that the problem may, indeed, have more than one correct answer.

Mathematics leaders must provide analysis experiences for teachers in a nonthreatening way, using hypothetical problems like those above. When the problems are not from their own classrooms, teachers can freely discuss what they think is happening. As ideas are shared, mathematics leaders should press teachers to select strategies to address the errors. What might teachers do in future lessons to help clarify students' understandings? In the case of the example questions, for instance, teachers might recommend scaffolding vocabulary, emphasizing various formats, or checking for specific details as well as general concepts in the summary of the lesson. But to gather more accurate information, teachers need to talk to students.

If mathematics leaders are engaged in benchmark assessments but have not developed a classroom visit form, the example below may still be used effectively with teachers. Even though teachers will not have feedback on student and teacher actions occurring in classrooms, they still can discuss instructional strategies and anticipated results, based on some of the benchmark results.

For example, let us assume that the following problem was given on a benchmark assessment with the result that fifty percent of the students answered the problem incorrectly and distracter choice "C" was the most commonly chosen incorrect answer.

Maria had $7.01 to spend for lunch. When she arrived at Café-to-Go, she noticed the following prices. A hamburger was $4.76, a cheeseburger and fries were $6.85, and a chef salad was $4.50. What is the range of prices for these lunch items?

    A. $2.35   B. $5.37   C. $2.51   D. $5.78

Following are dialogue starters that teachers might use to elicit information from students concerning the students' thinking about this problem. A teacher might begin by saying, "Students, I want you to look at the problem on the overhead. This problem is from the test you took last week. Across our district about half of you correctly answered this problem. In this example you see that the answer choice is A. Work with a partner and then be able to explain to me whether you think this is the correct response."

After a suitable period the teacher would then ask

"Who is willing to offer an answer? Is A the correct one or not?"

"Why do you think it is the correct one? (or incorrect one?)"

"Who has another thought or opinion?"

Next the teacher might say, "Answer A is correct. But the most frequently chosen incorrect choice was C. Work with your partner to tell me why you think this incorrect answer was chosen so often."

After some thinking and discussion time for the students, the teacher would ask

"How do you think the problem was answered to get C?"

"What do you think caused this confusion?"

"What activity in class would have helped correct this confusion before the test?"

These types of assessment discussions with students should be limited in scope and highlight only examples of problems that emphasize conceptual confusion that teachers want to correct immediately. Teacher teams can best identify selected items to discuss with input from mathematics leaders. The purposes of such classroom discussions are to

- clarify students' reasoning,
- identify instructional strengths and weaknesses,
- locate students' misconceptions,
- identify item bias or errors, and
- target concepts that need scaffolding or additional instruction.

If more information is wanted or needed, small groups of students can be pulled together and led through a similar process during a tutorial session.

What if teachers decided in the preceding example that students did not understand the statistical concept of range? Without realizing that extraneous data were the culprit or that students had not read the problem carefully, they might spend another class day or more reteaching how to find the range of the data. Unless teachers identify students' misconceptions and how they were arrived at, and take steps to correct them, they are likely to find that students will continue to make the same errors.

BUILDING TRUST

Initially, teachers generally distrusted benchmark assessments and worried about how data may be used (Reeves, 2006). Benchmark assessments, while critical to improvement efforts, usually come as central-office mandates. Therefore, mathematics leaders must use caution and display empathy at the start of the improvement effort using benchmarks to save hours of frustration and hard feelings later. The main purpose for benchmark assessments is student improvement over time. Collaborative, collegial teams offer an effective way for leaders to build trust among teachers regarding the use of benchmark data and to give teachers a real voice in the improvement process (Short & Greer, 2002).

It will be well to remember that some mathematics leaders have authority to evaluate, but most do not. In either case, teachers' previous experiences with evaluation are likely to affect both leaders' and teachers' attitudes toward supportive data. Principals, in particular, struggle with the dual role of gathering data for both evaluation and support. Teachers often have difficulty distinguishing between the two, especially if they have experienced only evaluation. Developing trust will be key to getting teachers on board with efforts to improve student performance by using data to shape instructional practices.

What Are Leaders Expected to Do?

Mathematics leaders must exhibit a high degree of honesty. They must not make promises that they do not have authority to keep. They must maintain effective communication with principals and other administrators who may have very different understandings and ideas about classroom visits and benchmark assessments. Mathematics leaders also may need to deal with changes in school leadership while an improvement initiative is under way. For instance, a new principal may arrive on the scene with ideas and plans for improving student achievement that are different from those of his or her predecessor.

Trust is one of the most important attributes for mathematics leaders to establish. Maintaining teacher confidentiality and operating from a position of support will help leaders gain trust. Building and maintaining that trust will be a significant factor in empowering teachers (Short & Greer, 2002).

Leaders Build Trust

Balancing various data collection methods and purposes is a challenging task. Mathematics leaders must clearly distinguish between evaluative and supportive data collection. Those who cross the line between the two purposes without a clear reason will sow seeds of distrust among teachers. And telling them "not to worry" will not solve the resulting problems. Short and Greer (2002) comment,

> Trust building is a slow process that requires disclosure, authenticity of work and action, follow through in meeting others' needs, respect for diversity, enabling teachers to take action in risk-taking environments without fear of reprisal, and basic ethical actions that demonstrate a concern for the well-being of others. (p. 159)

Mathematics leaders also must establish a positive, collegial relationship with principals. They will need to establish regular meetings to share information about the improvement initiatives. But they cannot be conduits to provide "inside" information about specific teachers. This role would eventually lead to distrust by both teachers and principals. On the other hand, leaders must be prepared to answer principals' questions candidly and provide timely information about improvement efforts. Following is a practical example of a pitfall that mathematics leaders would do well to avoid when discussing improvement initiatives with principals. The scenario goes like this:

During a conversation the principal asks the mathematics leader, "What do you think of Ms. Jones?" The mathematics leader immediately gives an evaluation—good or bad—about Ms. Jones in an attempt to sound informed and to be seen as helpful. If the report is positive the mathematics leader feels that he or she has been supportive of Ms. Jones. This might seem to be innocuous, but it is a mistake. The mathematics leader should instead turn the question back to the principal by asking, "Are you concerned about Ms. Jones?" At this point the conversation might go in several directions. For instance, the principal might say, "No, she's new and I was just curious," or "Yes, I walked by her room the other day and it was very loud," or even "A parent called to complain about a grade, and I haven't had a chance to visit with Ms. Jones yet."

> *In response to one of the last two responses the mathematics leader might be tempted to ask, "What can I do to help?" However, this response clearly opens the mathematics leader to taking on tasks outside his or her responsibility and ultimately will undermine teachers' trust. Instead, the mathematics leader should again turn the question back to the principal, saying, "What are you planning to do?" The principal might respond in various ways, but the most likely are "I need to go back and check on her" or "I need to get to her class."*

The mathematics leader now has an opportunity to suggest classroom visits. If the principal is seeking evaluative information on Ms. Jones, then he or she should conduct such a visit. If a classroom visit is intended to check for Ms. Jones' use of particular strategies, then a supportive classroom visit—or series of visits—should be suggested. The mathematics leader can perform these supportive visits.

The mathematics leader in this example should be similarly cautious in conversation with Ms. Jones. It is not the leader's role to notify Ms. Jones of the principal's concerns. Confidentiality and discretion go both ways. If the leader were to convey the principal's concerns, it would undermine the principal's trust in the leader.

One effective communication strategy that builds trust in both teachers and principals is for the mathematics leader to suggest that the principal join the leader in taking an "implementation walk." Implementation walks, like the classroom visits discussed in Chapter 4, focus on strategies or programs being used in classrooms. After visiting several classrooms, mathematics leaders and principals share and discuss observed actions in relation to desired actions.

Implementation walks are excellent opportunities to remind principals about the mathematics curriculum and the improvement program being implemented. They also can serve to differentiate between evaluative and supportive data. One suggestion is to ask principals to focus on actions that students are taking, rather than on teachers' actions. This tends to help change an evaluative mindset. If a classroom visit form has been developed, mathematics leaders and principals can both complete the form and discuss their observations, which also can be shared with teachers.

Mathematics leaders who become frustrated with a seemingly slow process of change may be tempted to wish that they had evaluative power because then they could "get things moving—or else!" Of course, in reality this would be counterproductive for a couple of reasons. First, teachers need a source of supportive data so they can take risks without having to worry about a negative performance evaluation. If teachers dare not risk trying something new or different, then no changes can possibly take place. During change initiatives, teachers need someone who is by their side, not looking over their shoulder.

Second, truly effective principals empower teachers. Empowerment occurs only when power is shared. Transformational leadership, as it has been termed, invites staff into the management process (Marzano, Walters, & McNulty, 2005). Short and Greer (2002) state it this way:

> Power is thought to be an infinite commodity that is available to accomplish the goals and mission of the organization. To expand the amount of power, one involves additional persons in the decisions of the organization. . . . The saying "the principal gains power by giving it away" appears to sum up the process. (p. 14)

In maintaining a supportive role, mathematics leaders must manage data transparently, except when confidentiality issues are involved. Teachers need to know what data are collected and how data are organized. They also need to know which data are saved and where they are stored. At every opportunity, mathematics leaders should minimize teachers' identification. If teachers' names are not on the documents, then the information cannot end up in teachers' files as evaluative documentation.

As data are analyzed, mathematics leaders should encourage teachers to identify their needs as much as possible and to maintain the focus on improving students' learning by addressing factors that teachers control. Leaders need to be cautious in shaping suggestions. If mathematics leaders too often overrule teachers' recommendations or suggestions, then teachers will come to distrust leaders' attempts at involvement and empowerment. At the same time, leaders should not be passive or voiceless. Teachers cannot decide to throw out an adopted curriculum, for example. The goal for all must be to engender realistic, manageable change.

Resources That Leaders Can Use

School environments usually are direct results of the management styles of principals (Short & Greer, 2002). Processes that principals use to engage teachers in making decisions demonstrate whether teachers' opinions are valued and respected. This, in turn, determines the professional climate. Regardless of whether the climate is positive or negative, however, mathematics leaders must work to empower teachers within their sphere of influence.

Assessment principles are identified in the National Council of Teachers of Mathematics (2000) *Principles* and place a focus on feedback in order to enhance student learning. Data are used to inform instructional decisions. A similar emphasis is found in the National Council of Supervisors of Mathematics (2008) *PRIME Leadership Framework,* which also supports feedback used to enhance student learning.

7 Establishing Professional Learning Communities

Professional learning communities (PLCs) serve to sustain change initiatives and empower teachers. Mathematics leaders may find themselves in schools that have some form of PLC. If PLCs are in place, then the start of a mathematics achievement improvement effort is an excellent time to reevaluate, realign, and refocus them. If PLCs have not yet been created, then it is a good time to develop them.

Professional learning communities do not just happen. Mathematics leaders and teachers must work at developing a trusting, collegial environment. In this chapter we will help leaders

- develop deep understanding of, respect for, and support for collaboration;
- establish effective professional learning communities; and

- understand the need for reflective practice as an integral part of the PLC philosophy.

While learning communities can operate successfully in many settings, PLCs usually cannot be established and sustained without district-level support. To maintain this interest and support, there should be at least one advocate who is articulate and well informed about the principles and operations of various types of learning communities. That role often falls to mathematics leaders.

ESTABLISHING COLLABORATION

Teachers need to work in collaborative groups that provide time for articulating and clarifying lessons, assessing lesson delivery, and reflecting on the effects of lessons on student learning (DuFour, 2004). In their daily routines, teachers normally find it challenging to implement new lesson strategies, especially considering that change frequently must be undertaken with minimal assistance or support. After professional development training, teachers most often return to their classrooms expected to implement a new strategy without practical, hands-on experience. Teachers face the same students with the same textbooks and yet are expected to institute different instructional techniques. Clearly, more has to change than simply what is expected of teachers. One thing is how teachers not only acquire new information but also hone the skills to integrate it into practice.

What Are Leaders Expected to Do?

One of the primary realizations that mathematics leaders, principals, and central office personnel must come to is that one person—namely, the classroom teacher—cannot institute change alone (Reeves, 2006). To begin, substantive change will happen only when others are invited into the process of making decisions. One mark of exceptional leaders is a creation of teams (Reeves, 2006). These teams, if they are to function properly, must have time to collaborate. But fulfilling the potential of collaboration involves more than simply arranging time for teachers to meet and engaging them in unstructured conversations.

Teachers do not do their best work, nor do students learn as much, without the benefits of collaboration (Stronge, 2007). Like students, when teachers work solely independently, their potential to institute significant change or improvement decreases. A similar decrease happens when only whole-group learning opportunities are provided. Whole-group faculty meetings and professional development workshops, for example, serve specific purposes. But these are large-group gatherings. They cannot be expected to develop the depths of trust and high degrees of information that are more likely to be achieved in small, collegial teams.

Learning communities are important to teacher empowerment, and mathematics leaders will be expected to be directly involved in establishing them along specific lines of intent. Short and Greer (2002) quote an earlier work that describes these intentions as follows:

> Short and Rinehart (1992) identified six empirically desired dimensions of teacher empowerment: involvement in decision-making, opportunity for professional growth, teacher status, teacher self-efficacy, autonomy, and teacher impact. (p. 150)

Each of these six aspects can be developed through collaboration within professional learning communities.

Leaders Help Establish Collaboration

We discussed the detrimental effects of teacher isolation previously. Mathematics leaders promote collegiality in order to combat the negative effects of isolation. Collegial relationships are deeper than and different from personal friendships or simple courtesy during professional interactions. Collegiality is developed, just as trust is developed, over time and with specific care and attention. Marzano (2003) points out that collegiality can be characterized by authentic interactions that are professional in nature. These interactions can be scheduled and organized under the guidance of mathematics leaders.

Mathematics leaders promote and support the formation of collaborative teacher groups with the goal of improving student learning and achievement. According to Reeves (2006),

> Without effective collaboration, five different teachers can simultaneously hold a dozen different ideas of what the word "proficient" means, with some teachers rewarding effort, attitude, and penmanship, while others focus on time management and cooperation, and still others focus on academic content and written expression. (p. 104)

In forming PLCs, mathematics leaders must work closely with teachers to develop the skills they will need to achieve effective teams.

Effective collaborative groups operate with a sense of efficacy. Teachers believe that they control the conditions for student learning. Mathematics leaders must respect, nurture, and support this belief. Furthermore, leaders cannot initiate a team-building process in order to push their own improvement plans. Reeves reminds us, "Collaboration implies shared decision making and a willingness to concede one's own agenda" (p. 51). Teachers will recognize and resent leaders' false or superficial involvement efforts. Teachers' involvement in change efforts is directly related to the degree to which they feel that their input has an effect and that administrative desire for their input was genuine (Short & Greer, 2002).

Authenticity is a characteristic that leaders (and others in authority) must demonstrate to develop fully functional PLCs. At the root, mathematics leaders must recognize, in the words of Reeves (2006), "Employees in any organization are volunteers. We can compel their attendance and compliance, but only they can volunteer their hearts and minds" (p. 52). When teachers volunteer their hearts and minds, they are empowered.

Resources That Leaders Can Use

As mathematics leaders think about collaboration, they should begin a serious campaign to involve those individuals who need to be part of the team effort. Mathematics leaders need to gather research to support collaborative structures and ensure that it is available for study by those who will be members of the PLC. The National Council of Teachers of Mathematics offers "Research Briefs and Clips" on its website at www.nctm.org. This is an excellent starting point. Website visitors will find research results on topics such as student learning, algebra, curriculum, effective instruction, and formative assessment. Other organizations also publish books discussing professional learning communities. Research on achievement data is available through the National Assessment of Educational Progress (NAEP), Trends in International Mathematics and Science Study (TIMSS), and other sources. In using theses resources, however, mathematics leaders would do well to provide condensed research summaries so that important aspects can be highlighted. Mathematics leaders also should take opportunities to discuss collaboration with others at all levels of a school and district. Information and insights can come from unexpected sources as leaders encourage the collaborating teachers to discuss strategies, data, and student achievement.

BUILDING COMMUNITY

If teachers are expected to implement effective instructional strategies, they need time, support, and the power to act. According to DuFour (2004),

A comprehensive study of the restructuring movement in education led to two significant conclusions: (1) a strong professional learning community was critical to gains in student achievement, and (2) the principals who led those learning communities were committed to empowering their teachers. (p. 141)

This structural shift is a foundation for changing and improving instructional strategies.

Collaborative structures, as we noted in the preceding section, are essential for developing strong professional learning communities. Planning lessons together, for example, is time well spent. Through regular dialogue focused on student achievement, teachers will be better prepared to adopt new strategies. Collaboration also helps to refine, improve, and sustain efforts (Schmoker, 1999). Within these teams, leaders provide a framework for content and outcomes and then structure opportunities for teachers to develop and present lessons. Teachers are encouraged to create ways to support one another when incorporating new strategies in the classroom practice.

What Are Leaders Expected to Do?

Professional learning communities are different from working teams assigned to collaborate on a specific task or project, such as benchmark assessments or materials for a particular instructional unit. These narrowly focused team efforts are invaluable and serve the purpose of tapping into teachers' expertise and experiences. Indeed, such teams can be used early on to pave the way for PLCs that have a broader focus. Mathematics leaders need to be able to distinguish between working teams and PLCs. The following characteristics may be helpful to keep in mind. Professional learning communities

- concentrate on student achievement based on examining a common curriculum, common assessments, and supportive data;
- require a level of engagement and trust that sometimes is not established early in a change process;
- may require extra effort to garner support from school administrators because of previous failed efforts or simply lack of understanding;
- cannot be a "break-point" for mathematics leaders because if resistance to a PLC makes forming one unfeasible, there still are other steps that leaders can take to improve teaching and learning; and
- take time, energy, and commitment, which may be limited and must be used wisely as mathematics leaders decide where the real leverage points for change are located and act accordingly.

Given these considerations, PLCs are not easy to build and maintain, though they certainly are worthy of mathematics leaders' efforts. One point that should help leaders is to understand clearly the central goals of effective PLCs. Youngs and King (2002) state them this way:

> A strong schoolwide professional community is characterized by (a) shared goals for student learning; (b) meaningful collaboration among faculty members; (c) in-depth inquiry into assumptions, evidence, and alternative solutions to problems; and (d) opportunities for teachers to exert influence over their work. (p. 646)

Each characteristic should be carefully considered.

Leaders Help Teachers Build Community

The role of mathematics leaders in the context of PLCs can be described by five functions: (1) invite teachers, (2) analyze data, (3) train teachers, (4) structure community, and (5) monitor functions. These can be further detailed as follows:

1. Mathematics leaders invite teachers to participate in professional learning communities. This invitation begins with the sharing of information and research about PLCs. After carefully reviewing this information, teachers are ready to form groups. This step can be facilitated fairly easily in smaller mathematics departments because all of the teachers may be able to participate in the same PLC. Once the group has been formed, mathematics leaders can establish clear goals, initial tasks, and explicit expectations of the PLC (Short & Greer, 2002). The goals should be supported by research and broad enough for teachers to participate in setting them. A primary goal must be advancing and supporting a strong relationship between program adherence and student achievement (Youngs & King, 2002).

2. Data analysis is an important function of PLCs and an appropriate place to begin work. Mathematics leaders need to provide data on classroom visits and benchmark assessments for teachers to analyze. Mathematics leaders can best promote collaboration and reflective inquiry by allocating adequate time for teachers to meet on a consistent basis to study these data (Youngs & King, 2002). Effective teachers invite feedback and critiques from others, but this skill does not develop without effort (Stronge, 2007).

3. Mathematics leaders must provide initial training to ensure that teachers understand their responsibilities in a PLC. It is important

to distribute responsibilities in a way that promotes collective efficacy (Marzano, Walters, & McNulty, 2005). Teachers also need to develop listening skills and skills in using clarifying and probing statements to check for student understanding (Short & Greer, 2002). These skills help teachers engage in meaningful professional conversations within the collegial setting of the PLC. Mathematics leaders will need to model these skills themselves as they train teachers. Another training topic will be problem identification and solution, in which teachers will have a high level of involvement. This in turn will give teachers a greater sense of influence over factors that affect student learning. Effective learning communities are built through many types of ongoing conversations in which the role of leaders is encouragement and support (Short & Greer, 2002).

4. Functioning PLCs help build school leaders (Marzano, Walters, & McNulty, 2005). "Structuring community" refers to assigning jobs and rotating responsibilities among members of a PLC. Teacher leaders should be chosen to take responsibility for setting agendas, scheduling and conducting meetings, keeping records, and other functions. These jobs can rotate on an agreed-on schedule. All team members should work to keep the group focused, but establishing a signal that can be used by any member to indicate that the group has moved off course during a meeting can be helpful. The signal could be raising a red card or a ringing a small bell.

5. Mathematics leaders monitor the functioning of professional learning communities at three points:

   A. During meetings through participation or minutes
   B. After meetings through classroom visits
   C. Periodically by reviewing student achievement results on benchmarks and other assessments

This monitoring process is not done as evaluation nor is it done secretively. Teachers need to understand the process of monitoring and accept feedback as they do other supportive data. Mathematics leaders cannot attend, nor should they attend, every PLC meeting. Teams need time to work together on their own. Mathematics leaders should attend enough meetings to be credible and read meeting minutes to stay knowledgeable. When teachers decide to institute new practices, mathematics leaders should visit classrooms and observe the action. Leaders can serve as a "third eye," helping to link team decisions with classroom implementation.

As PLCs continue to develop, mathematics leaders need to mentor teacher leaders by meeting with them on their own. During these meetings team leaders should have candid conversations about problems or concerns that may be emerging from PLC meetings. Mathematics leaders should be prepared to help teacher leaders understand and deal with group dynamics. Though they probably will not be available to answer every question, mathematics leaders should serve to broker information by locating resources for teacher leaders. Such meetings also should include principals on a regular schedule, especially during the initial development of a PLC.

An important purpose of learning communities is to focus on increasing student achievement. Teachers need to see a definite link between outcomes of a PLC and results of student learning.

Resources That Leaders Can Use

There are many resources for mathematics leaders to use in planning, developing, and supporting professional learning communities. Leaders may want to begin with some of the resources referenced throughout this section. There also are many articles carried by education journals that will assist mathematics leaders in initiating conversations with staff. *Whatever It Takes: How Professional Learning Communities Respond When Kids Don't Learn*, by Rick DuFour (2004) and his colleagues includes very useful resources. Also, *The Adoptive School: A Sourcebook for Developing Collaborative Groups*, by Garmston and Wellman (1999) provides helpful information about group dynamics and functions.

FACILITATING REFLECTION

Reflecting on classroom actions facilitates changes in behavior (Short & Greer, 2002). By reflecting on lessons, teachers identify instructional strategies that are effective for selected content objectives. According to Williams (1996), "Schools need to support teachers by providing time for staff to share, collaborate, and discuss the impact of their teaching and assessment practices" (p. 90). Effective reflection requires the fuel of assessment and analysis of student work in order to be productive. Gathering this fuel would be an overwhelming task for one person, such as a mathematics leader. However, it can be accomplished through teamwork in a professional learning community.

What Are Leaders Expected to Do?

Mathematics leaders must understand the steps involved in a reflective process and be able to train teachers and teacher leaders in that process. York-Barr and colleagues (2001) summarize the key elements as follows:

> To be effective means to mentally wander through where you have been and try to make sense out of it. Reflection involves such habits or dispositions as:
>
> - Metacognition: Thinking about thinking and conducting an internal dialogue before, during, and after an event
> - Drawing forth cognitive and emotional information from several sources: visual, auditory, kinesthetic, and tactile
> - Acting on and processing the information—synthesizing, evaluating
> - Applying insights to contexts beyond the one in which they were learned. (p. xv)

These habits of reflection help teachers improve the act of teaching.

Teachers lead hectic lives that are not conducive to reflection (York-Barr, Sommers, Ghere, & Montie, 2001). As a result, if reflection is not practiced during professional learning community meetings, it is likely not to take place at all. Mathematics leaders must recognize first of all that reflective practice in groups is not necessarily comfortable. According to York-Barr and colleagues (2001), "There is a big shift from reflecting alone or with a partner to reflecting in a small group, such as a team or committee. While the potential impact of reflection increases, so does personal risk" (p. 14). Thus, patience and practice will be required.

Mathematics leaders can encourage teachers to talk about their classrooms by asking them to recount events that occurred recently. These conversations will be about common lessons. Teachers can discuss elements of a lesson that worked as planned, elements that had to be adjusted, and any parts of a lesson that were left out. After these narratives, teachers can begin to reflect on how they perceived students participating in a lesson. They also can discuss objectives that they felt students were successful in meeting or on which students fell short. Using information about events in classrooms, teachers are able to think about the process of teaching and instructional strategies that were effective or ineffective. This reflective practice will help teachers (and leaders) target strategies that can be introduced, improved, or eliminated to improve students' learning.

Resources That Leaders Can Use

The reflective process for mathematics leaders is one of listening, not speaking. Leaders need to have questions at their fingertips—questions that probe rather than direct or accuse. Teachers should not feel as though they are being "grilled" by mathematics leaders or feel the need to "guess" what mathematics leaders are thinking. Reflective sessions should feel safe; they should be secure opportunities for teachers to think carefully about their teaching practices and the student learning that is (or is not) happening in their classrooms.

Mathematics leaders should be prepared with non-threatening, open-ended questions designed to help teachers review their lessons, such as:

- What lesson did you teach?
- What did you want the students to be able to do?
- Did the lesson unfold as you had planned it to do?
- What were the strong points of the lesson—where you felt the students were really understanding?
- Do you think your students are ready to move ahead?
- If you could teach this lesson again, what would you do differently?
- Did some activities take longer than you anticipated?
- Were the activities the correct ones for the lesson?
- Did the students reach closure as you intended?
- What do you think other members of your mathematics staff need to hear about this topic?

These questions are merely a guide. Mathematics leaders must be careful listeners, prepared to take cues from teachers about which questions to ask and when to ask them.

Finally, professional learning communities can work to actualize the NCTM *Principles* and the NCSM *PRIME Leadership Framework,* emphasizing student learning directly related to curriculum, teaching, and assessment.

8 Fostering Professional Development

Continual learning and appropriate application of learning are hallmarks of effective schools (Kaser, Mundry, Stiles, & Loucks-Horsley, 2001). Mathematics leaders must be responsible for carefully orchestrating learning for mathematics teachers and support staff. This orchestrated delivery of professional development can take many forms.

In education, most professional development is done in a workshop setting. Teachers rarely are given choices about the type of professional development in which they can engage and consequently may have difficulty relating new knowledge to existing practice (Kaser et al., 2001). This approach to "teaching teachers" has not been highly successful and, indeed, may be responsible for many reform failures.

Just as modern research has identified approaches to improving student learning, similar advances have been made in the field of adult learning. "Best practices," which we review in this chapter, are becoming cornerstones for effective professional development. Mathematics leaders need to draw on these practices when designing, developing, and delivering professional development for mathematics teachers.

STRUCTURING EFFECTIVE PROFESSIONAL DEVELOPMENT

Effective professional development must provide avenues for new learning, ideally about practice elements that can transfer directly into classroom settings. Such professional development should help teachers by building both content and pedagogical knowledge.

Teachers need to have a voice in the form and content of professional development and should be able to see a clear relationship between what they are to learn and what they need to know in order to increase student achievement. Furthermore, professional development should maintain a consistent focus on student learning, be sustained over time, and be easy to embed into routine classroom practice (Loucks-Horsley, Love, Stiles, Mundry, & Hewson, 2003).

What Are Leaders Expected to Do?

Mathematics leaders have responsibilities to guide teacher learning, promote competence, and support implementation of effective teaching strategies.

Professional development often is seen as the panacea for education's woes. Rarely is a problem in education identified without professional development being offered as *the* solution. The difficulty arises with a simple word *the*. Professional development is not *the* solution, but it is, or should be, part of *a* solution. Change initiatives often begin with some form of professional development. Once an initiative or program has been undertaken and training conducted, there seems to be a general belief that implementation has somehow been completed. Little real thought tends to be given to monitoring implementation or assessing the effect of the initiative (Schmoker, 1999).

An all-too-common process for professional development follows four steps: 1) an initiative or program is selected (frequently by a top-down process); 2) teachers are informed of a decision and required to attend one to three days of training; 3) training is conducted using a format that ignores what educators know about effective instruction, specifically adult learning; and 4) teachers are provided information in whole-group settings with little regard to real application in their classrooms. Typically, the result of this process is no substantive change in teachers' practices. Mathematics leaders need to break this model.

Leaders Help Structure Professional Development Opportunities

Professional development should not follow a deficit model of learning, in which teachers are simply presented with more and more information on the assumption that, as a result, their actions and beliefs will change. To be truly effective, the approach to professional development must be expanded. This is not to say that certain aspects of traditional approaches cannot be of value. But they must be amplified and supplemented if professional development is to have the desired effect of changing teachers' beliefs and practices and improving students' learning. While we take up professional development as the final stage in our mathematics leadership model, it should be recognized that mathematics leaders may need to make professional development the first stage in the continuous improvement cycle of teacher learning that improves student achievement.

A typical thesaurus will list such synonyms for *development* as *growth, expansion, progress, advance, increase, maturity, enlargement,* and *improvement.* These words convey the essence of professional development. According to Kaser and colleagues (2001), professional development can be further characterized in the following ways:

- It supports teachers in making explicit connections between what they do and what their students learn.
- It is designed to build a learning community in which all take responsibility for learning over time and the staff works collegially to share knowledge, insight, and experience.
- It empowers the staff to design, conduct, and follow through on their own learning.
- It provides follow-up support and time for practice and reflection.
- It establishes a safe environment in which the staff can take risks without fear of failure or ridicule.
- It holds the staff accountable for their learning and its impact on outcomes.
- It continuously monitors and evaluates the successes, difficulties, and failures of the new approach. (p. 133)

It is noteworthy that this list encompasses the developmental stages articulated in preceding chapters. Effective professional development must be interrelated with the other aspects of improvement that we have detailed. The various developmental stages detailed in this book hover in the background of these characteristics. In other words, effective professional development cannot be achieved without recommendations from the other stages operating in some capacity.

Mathematics leaders must consider how professional development can build on assets already in place, such as a curriculum guide, instructional strategies, data from assessments and visits, and established professional learning communities. Leaders should understand that effective teachers will be committed to a process of personal learning, and this personal learning, often accomplished through professional development, will necessarily connect positively to student achievement (Stronge, 2007). Mathematics leaders must "clearly connect professional development to student learning and, more particularly, to closing persistent achievement gaps between rich and poor and white and African American and Hispanic" (Loucks-Horsley et al., 2003, p. 1).

Mathematics leaders also should remember the challenge of engaging and empowering staff: "As a dimension of empowerment, professional growth refers to teachers' perceptions that the school in which they work provides them with opportunities to grow and develop professionally, learn continuously, and expand their own skills through the work life of the school" (Short & Greer, 2002, p. 152).

Even though teachers may learn how to do something differently, that new knowledge will not automatically transfer to practice. Teachers—and mathematics leaders—have mental models, the images that we all carry in our minds about ourselves, other people, and institutions (Senge et al., 2000). These models can limit peoples' abilities to change. Mental models exist below the surface, and therefore influence our actions without ever coming to the light to be examined (Senge et al., 2000).

According to Kennedy (2005), the idea of mental models can be tapped so that, through professional development, teachers are assisted in forming mental lesson scripts to use when planning and delivering lessons. These scripts influence lesson presentation and flow. More importantly, Kennedy notes, these lesson scripts can affect the momentum of a lesson, the process of "keeping things moving along, avoiding distractions, making sure everyone is on the same page, and so forth" (p. 46). If mental models and mental scripts determine activities and events that occur in a classroom, then to enact change mathematics leaders will need to work on altering teachers' existing mental models. Professional development can bring to light teachers' mental frameworks and then work to substitute different models and scripts.

To begin, mathematics leaders must recognize a strong link between lesson planning and lesson delivery. There also is a strong link between lesson materials and lesson delivery. Lessons planned with specific activities and strategies and with appropriate supporting materials are likely to be presented as planned. Professional learning communities and articulated curricula are tools that mathematics leaders can use to facilitate the teacher empowerment that will propel appropriate planning and subsequent instruction.

Much professional development occurs in PLCs. However, professional learning communities cannot serve as an entire professional development program. When planning classroom instruction, teachers must recognize that students will need a variety of approaches and strategies in order to learn. This also is true for adult learners.

Resources That Leaders Can Use

Mathematics leaders must think about the forms of professional development currently used in their schools or districts. Some of these probably will be outside their control. Principals may be charged with providing some professional development opportunities, and most principals feel a need, or are required, to hold regularly scheduled faculty meetings in which some professional development may take place. Mathematics leaders probably will have to live within this structure while trying to improve it.

For professional development scheduled by others, mathematics leaders need to seek to understand the intended outcomes, how development sessions will be (or have been) conducted, and consider whether they may be able to follow up with more targeted training. For example, mathematics leaders may discover that incorporating higher-order thinking skills in the general curriculum has been a major initiative of the district. As a result, teachers in the district are scheduled for two days of training prior to the start of school to learn how to incorporate higher-order thinking strategies into their lessons. Mathematics leaders might take this opportunity to get a list of intended strategies, find articles that explain these strategies in mathematics teaching contexts, and then build related professional development for mathematics teachers that sharpens the focus provided by the more general inservice program.

There are other types of effective professional development that mathematics leaders may encourage, deliver, or support. Depending on their job responsibilities, professional relationships, district or school organizations, supervisory expectations, and other factors, mathematics leaders probably will be able to find a variety of ways to deliver, support, or enhance adult learning. New forms also merit consideration, such as the e-workshop, an electronic online workshop delivered through the Internet and telephone. The National Council of Teachers of Mathematics now offers several topics through this method.

MENTORING AND COACHING

Two other approaches to professional development are mentoring and coaching. These have similarities and differences, and mathematics leaders will need to find the correct combination that works for them and the teachers they want to mentor or coach. Coaching and mentoring both may operate within or outside professional learning communities. Coaching often can be thought of as a one-on-one approach to teacher improvement and is usually conducted between peers (Loucks-Horsley et al., 2003). By contrast, mentoring usually pairs a more experienced teacher with a less experienced one.

Coaching and mentoring both involve planning, presenting, and reflecting. Coaching is a supportive role, not an evaluative role. Even though mathematics coaches may be assigned to the duty and no longer have, or have only limited, classroom teaching responsibilities, there usually is not sufficient positional distance between teacher and coach for the coach's role to be viewed as supervisory. Mathematics leaders may serve as coaches or mentors or may supervise coaches or mentors.

Understanding Coaching

Effective coaching requires mutual respect. It is not the function of coaches to tell teachers what to teach or how to teach it. Rather, the two individuals in the coaching relationship should develop a lesson or series of lessons together. Each will bring ideas and suggestions to be carefully considered and valued. Once the lesson has been planned, it should be more powerful than either person might have created alone.

Coaches may or may not be present for the lessons when they are taught. However, they should occasionally be present to observe and give firsthand feedback, rather than rely solely on the teachers' perception in follow-up conversations. When present, coaches should be active participants, not directors; that role should be left to the teachers. They may still circulate and interact with students. By doing so coaches may create a less "structured" appearance to coaching that otherwise might look like an official observation. In other cases, coaches might look for agreed-on skills, about which the teacher wants specific feedback. General observation should not be the goal of coaches when in the classroom.

After a lesson has been taught, the teacher and coach need time to visit as soon as it can reasonably be scheduled. Debriefing should be collegial and cordial. A teacher's perceptions of how a lesson went and what students learned are important to the coaching process. The best case is that coach and teacher basically agree on the strong points of a lesson and the less successful ones. Then they can put their heads together and decide on what needs to be done in the future. When there is disagreement, the coach should be prepared to make suggestions and recommendations about parts of the lesson that he or she believes did not go well.

Coaching can be a shared team experience that rotates among staff members. Lessons may be planned in a community setting, and then individual teachers can volunteer to teach a lesson for feedback. Coaching also may occur in subgroups of the staff. For example, three Algebra I teachers might want to work in a coaching situation.

One approach to coaching involves video-recording lessons for teachers to self-reflect on their teaching. Recorded lessons can be beneficial but should be used with care. Confidentiality can be important for both the teacher and the students in the class. Therefore, access to the video should be controlled, and recordings should be erased or destroyed after use. One caveat for mathematics leaders is to be aware that some teachers become hypercritical when they see themselves onscreen. This can be detrimental to improvement, and leaders should guard against it.

Understanding Mentoring

An important distinction is worth making here about coaching versus mentoring. Mentoring typically is a one-on-one learning experience, in which there often is a perceived disparity in the extent of teaching experience of the two individuals. In most mentoring arrangements a more experienced teacher assists a less experienced teacher to "learn the ropes" of the school (Loucks-Horsley et al., 2003). Some schools have mentoring programs for all newly hired teachers (and other staff, including administrators). In other cases mentoring arrangements are developed as needed, usually when a teacher (of any level of experience) is perceived as having difficulty or needs professional guidance to improve his or her performance. Mathematics leaders may work to develop mentoring relationships, either through personal involvement or by making suitable arrangements between staff members.

While mentoring serves several valuable purposes, it may not have a dramatic effect on a classroom unless the same type of activities— planning, presenting, and reflecting—are included, as they are in coaching. If these activities are included, mentors are likely to play a more directive role in deciding what to teach and how to teach it than would be the case with a coach.

OTHER APPROACHES TO PROFESSIONAL DEVELOPMENT

Professional development also can take place in book study groups. Book studies provide opportunities for teachers and mathematics leaders to work together and are excellent for cooperative activities outside a professional learning community (Loucks-Horsley et al., 2003). While book studies—or article reviews—can occur within a PLC, they can operate outside them just as easily. Through book studies, teachers have opportunities not only to interact with teachers outside their team but also in cross-curricular areas. Book study groups can be formed with an expectation that a team or small group will read and study a book and then share what they learn with other staff, for example, at a faculty meeting. In other cases, the readers might write brief summaries or conduct training based on their reading.

Lesson study is another form for professional development. Lesson study has some similarities to coaching. The idea is to improve classroom teaching and learning through planning, presenting, and reflecting. In lesson study, one or a few lessons are planned and studied in a collaborative setting. The same lesson is repeatedly analyzed and improved over an extended time. Lesson study focuses on helping teachers refine instructional techniques; however, it also can provide lessons for use in a curriculum guide or other materials. Lesson study lessons typically are not used only by a coach and a teacher but by the mathematics staff (Loucks-Horsley et al., 2003).

Another possibility is that some teachers may need specific content training for areas of mathematics that are not in their background, such as probability and statistics, or they may need assistance understanding and using manipulatives or certain forms of technology. As teachers work with data from benchmarks or visits, mathematics leaders may notice that they draw conclusions and act on data as fact when only an inference can be drawn because a sample size is too small. In all of these instances, mathematics leaders will be charged with creating appropriate professional development.

Finally, teachers may require assistance to work with colleagues in unaccustomed ways. Kaser and colleagues (2001) put it this way: "Teachers need help in setting rules and responsibilities for working in teams. If team learning is to occur, several components must be in place" (p. 180). These components include:

- a task on which to focus and a reason for the group to work together,
- a facilitator to aid learning, and
- a set of ground rules for their conversation.

Everyone on a team must clearly understand the purpose of the team and how it will function. Team members need to be able to explain the actions they take and how these actions are intended to improve student learning. Team members also must recognize and understand the role of the team leader and other assigned positions and yet retain collective responsibility for an effectively functioning team.

Professional development is threaded through the NCTM *Principles* and the NCSM *PRIME Leadership Framework*. Appropriate professional development, as Loucks-Horsley and colleagues (2003) remark, "provides opportunities for teachers to build their content and pedagogical content knowledge and examine practice" (p. 44). Mathematics leaders must be critical agents for teachers, deeply understanding the mathematics curriculum and content and promoting effective classroom activities—all supported by high-quality professional development, which they may be charged to deliver personally.

Part III

Continuing the Work

9 Reflecting on How Students Learn Mathematics

Students learn mathematics by being actively engaged in the lessons (National Research Council, 2004). The degree to which students are engaged in lessons is directly related to the actions of mathematics teachers (National Council of Teachers of Mathematics, 2000). To truly be effective, these actions must be thoughtfully planned and presented. Engagement means that students participate: talk, record information, share thoughts and ideas, speculate, justify, and make sense of what they are doing. In all its forms, mathematics helps students make sense and find meaning in a physical world that often is difficult to understand.

Understanding how students learn and staying up to date on new research into learning are important skills for mathematics leaders. To answer the question, "How do students learn mathematics?" mathematics leaders must be able to answer several related questions:

- What mathematics must or should students learn?
- What methods and tools will be most effective in helping students learn?
- What does research say?
- How do students learn to become problem solvers?
- How do students learn to communicate mathematics?

In this chapter we will take up each of these questions in turn.

WHAT MATHEMATICS MUST OR SHOULD STUDENTS LEARN?

Mathematics educators agree that students must gain fundamental understanding of number sense and operations (arithmetic), algebra, geometry, measurement, probability, and data analysis to be informed citizens, to compete in a workforce that now demands advanced technology skills, and to be prepared for higher education. These content areas are referred to in the National Council of Teachers of Mathematics (2000) book, *Principles and Standards for School Mathematics*. However, even young children in daycare and preschool are learning mathematics, albeit on a very basic level. In these settings, children are exposed to number and geometry concepts through a variety of experiences. Additionally, home-use media, such as the Baby Einstein program (www.babyeinstein.com) of DVDs, CDs, and related products, are exposing infants, toddlers, and young children to mathematics in many ways.

Mathematics also is a language used in many forms: numbers representing quantities, data, and money; computation among those numbers; shapes and measurement of shapes. How students learn the language of mathematics is critical for teachers to understand, along with knowing what students have learned of mathematics before coming to them and what students can anticipate learning in future classes. Mathematics leaders must continually update team members on the latest research findings germane to curricula and instruction that will positively affect mathematics learning and achievement. Recent examples are statistics and probability courses and discrete mathematics courses, which have been established in a number of high schools. For statistics and probability, students are involved in analyzing data and creating statistical models. Discrete mathematics is a relatively new branch of mathematics dealing with objects that can assume only distinct, separated values rather than continuous. Topics in courses include combinatorics, graph theory, recurrence relations, and algorithms. Mathematics leaders need to know what mathematics are included in such courses and whether similar courses should be recommended in the school or district they serve.

WHAT METHODS AND TOOLS WILL BE MOST EFFECTIVE IN HELPING STUDENTS LEARN?

Mathematics leaders need to facilitate discussion among teachers about the myriad methods and tools at their disposal for helping students learn mathematics. Tools and methods are continually updated and refined. Teachers need to have more than a theoretical understanding of these tools; they must be able to use them with facility and be able to adapt them to fit the particular needs and requirements of their students, the course curriculum, and other factors.

By keeping current on research about how students learn, mathematics leaders position themselves to be able to translate generic learning research, such as that found in Marzano's 2001 article "Classroom Instruction That Works," into specific applications for mathematics classrooms. For example, Marzano identifies "recognizing similarities and differences" as a powerful learning strategy that teachers should help students learn how to use. It means helping students see and say what sets symbolic forms apart from word forms. What distinguishes one from another, for instance, in addition, subtraction, multiplication, or division? At the middle school level a similar type of example might be hierarchical relationships among various quadrilaterals. And at the high school level it might be parent functions and various transformations of those functions. In working with these concepts, teachers must carefully think about what is similar in the concept, symbolism, or term, and what is different. By helping students recognize similarities and differences, teachers increase positive learning transfer and decrease negative transfer.

Mathematical tools allow students to work with multiple representations. Tools facilitate looking for patterns or adding concrete opportunities to explore and solve problems. They help students organize their thinking by translating concrete, pictorial, numerical, symbolic or algebraic, graphical, and verbal or written expressions. There are many varieties of mathematical tools, such as counters, calculators, computers, protractors, rulers, shapes, tiles, base-ten blocks, unit squares, cubes, algebra tiles, and many more. None of these should be viewed as age-specific, though too often manipulatives tend to be used less with older than with younger students, something that those who teach older students might want to reconsider.

Teachers need to spend time discussing how various tools can best be used to emphasize a desired concept. Which characteristics of a tool can help students better learn a concept, and which characteristics might interfere with learning? For example, when young children are working with counters (a concrete representation) to show addition and subtraction, they can place five counters on a desk and either "add to" or "subtract from" the pile. The students can say, "Five counters plus three more counters are eight counters." The same verbal interaction works for subtraction. Symbolic representation can be introduced using this type of concrete representation for small numbers so that as students encounter larger numbers and more advanced computations, they will transition to the symbolic with relative ease.

WHAT DOES RESEARCH SAY?

The mathematics that students need to learn today is complex. It is more than merely basic operations and rules for computation, which might have sufficed for most of the population a century ago but is no longer sufficient. Aspects of problem solving, reasoning, and communication are now included in mathematics education research agendas. In this section, we highlight research related to important principles that mathematics leaders need to understand in order to assist teachers.

In their 2003 book *Helping Children Learn Mathematics*, Robert E. Reys and colleagues set down ten principles based on what we know about learning mathematics (pp. 152–154). The implications of these offer a perspective from which to view research. Jerry Johnson (2000) summarized mathematics education research in *Teaching and Learning Mathematics: Using Research to Shift from the "Yesterday" Mind to the "Tomorrow" Mind*, and several points from this work are cited under the corresponding principles, along with a sampling of other references.

Principle 1: Students should be actively involved in learning mathematics. According to Sowell (1989), mathematics achievement is increased through the long-term use of concrete instructional materials, and students' attitudes toward mathematics are improved when they have instruction with concrete materials provided by teachers knowledgeable about their use. Some specific actions include the following:

- Using base-ten blocks in activities for learning helps students construct meaningful relationships (Hiebert, 1988; Mason, 1987).
- Using base-ten blocks helps students improve their understanding of place value, their accuracy when computing multi-digit addition and subtraction problems, and their verbal explanations of the trading/regrouping involved in these problems (Fuson & Briars, 1990; Fuson, 1986).
- The developmental level of many secondary students necessitates experiences with both concrete and pictorial representations of mathematical concepts (Driscoll, 1983).

Principle 2: Mathematics learning is a developmental process. According to Bergeron and Herscovics (1990), a prerequisite for a child's learning to count is acquisition of and fluency with the number-word sequence (one, two, . . .). Other points in the developmental process are as follows:

- Students need a good understanding of the concept of both a fraction and fraction equivalence before being introduced to computation situations and procedures involving fractions (Bezuk & Bieck, 1993; Mack, 1993).

- A weak understanding of place value will cause students to have a difficult time understanding decimals (Threadgill-Sowder, 1984).
- Student understanding of the concept of a variable provides the basis for the transition from arithmetic to algebra and is necessary for the meaningful use of all advanced mathematics (Schoenfeld & Aracavi, 1988).

Principle 3: Mathematics learning should build on previous learning. Lampert (1992) offers the example that performing division with any approach, including the long-division algorithm, requires proportional reasoning, which in turn requires students to understand numbers and the use of numbers in counting.

Principle 4: Communication is an integral part of mathematics learning. Bishop (1985) points out that both teachers and students must be involved if student communication about mathematics is to be successful. Additionally, negotiation of the meanings of symbols and words may be required. Other aspects of communication include such ideas as:

- Writing in a mathematical context helps students improve their mathematical understanding because it promotes reflection, clarifies their thinking, and provides a product that can initiate group discourse (Rose, 1989).
- Students need to discuss and reflect on connections between mathematical ideas (Hiebert & Carpenter, 1992).
- Mathematical discussion should be a daily part of classroom activity (Ball & Wilcox, 1989).

Principle 5: Good and interesting questions facilitate mathematics learning. Brown and Walter (1983, 1993) comment that an important component of problem solving, and fundamental to any mathematical activity, is problem posing.

Principle 6: Multi-embodiment aids learning in mathematics. Several writers refer to the idea that students need exposure to a variety of multiplication models (repeated addition, rectangular array, area) (English & Halford, 1995; Bell, Greer, Mangn, & Grimison, 1989). Other points include the following ideas:

- The area model is preferred over the set model as students construct an understanding of the concept of a fraction (English & Halford, 1995; Hope & Owens, 1987).
- Multiple representations of a shape, created in a computer environment, help students generalize their conceptual image of that shape in any size or orientation (Shelton, 1985).

Principle 7: Metacognition affects mathematics learning. An environment in which students build a "personal relationship" with mathematics is needed. Within this environment three elements are necessary, according to D'Ambrosio (1995),

- students need to engage in authentic mathematical inquiries,
- students must act like mathematicians as they explore ideas and concepts, and
- students need to negotiate the meaning of, and the connections among, these mathematical ideas with other students in the class.

Principle 8: Teachers' attitudes influence mathematics learning. A couple of sources make the point that warm and supportive teachers are more effective than critical teachers (Tikunoff, Berliner, & Rist, 1975; Rosenshine & Furst, 1971). Additionally, a critical ingredient in the building of an environment that promotes problem solving and makes students feel comfortable about their mathematics is the attitude of the mathematics teacher (Yackel, Cobb, Wood, Wheatley, & Merkel, 1990).

Principle 9: Mathematics anxiety is influenced by how mathematics is learned. The development of positive attitudes about mathematics is linked to the direct involvement of students in activities that include both high-quality mathematics and communication with significant others within a clearly defined community, such as a classroom (Van Oers, 1996).

Principle 10: Forgetting is a natural aspect of learning, but retention can be aided. An overriding theme throughout the research literature is that students learn mathematics best when they are interested, excited about what they are doing, and actively engaged in the learning activities. A key feature is activities or tasks that require higher-order thinking or problem-solving skills (Aschbacher, 1991). This is equally true for teachers learning new ways to plan and teach. Mathematics leaders need to ensure that all mathematics activities, from developing a curriculum to professional development, draw upon and use appropriate research on learning (Wiley, 2009, p. 152–154).

HOW DO STUDENTS LEARN TO BECOME PROBLEM SOLVERS?

Knowledge of mathematics coupled with the ability to apply mathematical skills to solve problems can be an empowering force for students. Becoming problem solvers in mathematics classrooms is a goal listed by most states and local districts in their curriculum documents. The extension of this problem-solving ability to other nonmathematics situations is critical for our society. At the college level, evidence that problem solving in mathematics is important arises when recruiters hire graduates who are mathematics majors with known problem-solving abilities for business careers over business majors who may not have similar problem-solving skills.

Over the years, teachers have assumed that problem-solving ability was tied to an ability to perform paper-and-pencil calculations. Teachers' and students' time was spent trying to remediate those who lacked this ability. Basing remediation on a premise that mathematics is linear and hierarchical and therefore must be taught in a prescribed order—rote skills first—left problem solving until later. However, research shows that repeating the same uninteresting tasks in the same unimaginative way is not effective when it comes to teaching students to be problem solvers.

The term "problem solving" itself has caused problems, with many educators still focusing on the terms such as "story problems" and "verbal problems" as synonymous with problem solving. Mathematics leaders must help classroom teachers understand problem solving in deeper contexts. As discussed in Chapter 5, problem solving is a group activity that requires students to gather data, organize data, make predictions, offer solutions, and justify their thinking. These actions increase understanding. According to the National Research Council (2002), "Knowledge learned with understanding provides a foundation for remembering or reconstructing mathematical facts and methods for solving new and unfamiliar problems, and for generating new knowledge" (p. 11). This is a far cry from merely doing word problems.

There is nothing wrong with putting mathematical problems into a word format that gives students a context in which the mathematics might arise. However, teachers need to be astute in analyzing and selecting these story problems in order to ensure appropriate mathematics learning. Solving problems is more involved than simply extracting numbers from a word problem or looking for keywords to indicate an operation. For some students, these approaches may reinforce a suspicion that mathematics is merely a trick, and it is their job to find the trick.

For example, when students are presented a lesson on three-digit addition and then given word problems to solve, they often find that they do not actually have to read the problem. They can look for numbers and add. Such a lesson usually is followed by one using three-digit subtraction. Students follow the same general process of locating the numbers and then subtracting the smaller number from the larger one without reading or attempting to understand the context. Then, when given a mix of problems in addition and subtraction, students do not think about the mathematics but look only for visual cues. They do not factor in the idea of extraneous data or unimportant information and so can miss the fact that their answer makes no sense. As more complex problems are introduced—for example, when students come to negative integers—the process falls apart completely, but bad habits have already become entrenched. Teachers must help students understand that problem solving is directly related to effort and persistence rather than innate ability. Mathematics helps make sense of the world, and developing the ability to solve problems of all sorts is the ultimate goal.

HOW DO STUDENTS LEARN TO COMMUNICATE MATHEMATICS?

As with language acquisition of any kind, students need opportunities to practice speaking, writing, reading, and listening mathematically. To be fluent with mathematics vocabulary, students need to use correct words for various mathematical ideas, whether they are talking or writing. Vocabulary knowledge increases with use, and incomplete or misunderstood vocabulary can seriously hamper students' understanding.

Mathematics teachers, especially in middle and high school, often feel that they are not responsible for teaching students to read or write. While this may be true for some of the skills students need to acquire in language arts, it is not true for mathematics. If mathematics teachers do not teach students to read and write *in mathematics,* then who will? If mathematics helps students better understand the world, then they must be able to communicate this understanding.

Students need to articulate their understanding through speech or in a written form that makes their thinking visible. Learning mathematics terminology is more complex than simply keeping a vocabulary notebook or copying definitions. Communication also is more involved than being able to describe a process, such as, "I put down the five and carried the three." Students should be encouraged to express their ideas, reasoning, and justifications using correct mathematical language.

Students' vocabulary is increased when teachers emphasize using correct words during explanations. In early development of new terms teachers may want to emphasize words that reinforce meaning. For example, in elementary classes teachers may want to say, "Notice the triangle, the shape with three sides. . . ." In high school teachers may say, "Notice that the data are linear, all the points are on a line. . . ." Teachers at all levels may find that creating a "word wall," a display of new vocabulary words, can be helpful to the effort. Finally, teachers will want to preteach new vocabulary, accentuating similarities and differences to familiar words before using the new words in lessons.

With the continual progress being made in brain research and an increased understanding of student learning, mathematics education will evolve. While leaders cannot, nor should not, allow teachers to remain in a constant state of flux, it is very important for leaders to remain informed. Leaders are also charged with the responsibility of helping teachers remain informed and consistently advancing in their knowledge of the art of teaching and the science of learning mathematics.

10 Putting It All Together

We noted at the start of this book that achieving equity by closing the achievement gap is the ultimate goal in mathematics education. In the preceding chapters we outlined a leadership model to accomplish this goal. The developmental stages of this model are sequential, though not rigidly so, and highly interrelated. To be successful, mathematics leaders, whether responsible for one school or several, will need to undertake some version of the leadership process that we have described.

The leadership process is dynamic, continuous, and cyclical. Mathematics leaders must be prepared for a changing environment, including student population shifts, staff changes, advances in pedagogy and assessment, new research findings, and so on. Their role will be to address such changes positively in order to reorient improvement efforts and to maintain progress.

Some keywords resonate throughout this process. We have discussed *engaging* and *empowering* teachers in the art of teaching as a critical aspect of mathematics leaders' work. Leaders engage teachers by *articulating* mathematics content, by *implementing* a curriculum as designed, and by *supporting* teachers' use of *effective instructional practices*. Leaders empower teachers by providing *timely feedback*, working in *professional learning communities*, and providing worthwhile *professional development*.

There is an adage: "A chain is only as strong as its weakest link." One way to reflect on the developmental stages of the leadership model is to consider each stage as a link. Each link depends on the next as well as on all the others to construct and maintain a strong chain—in this case, a strong mathematics program. The strength metaphor also works well in another way. Mathematics leaders should build on their school's or district's strengths, not weaknesses. If program implementation is strong but based on a misaligned curriculum, then a mathematics leader's work is, first, to maintain and further strengthen the positive aspects of implementation and, second, to address misalignment issues. If the district holds one-shot inservice programs, at least time is being devoted to some form of professional development. That is a strength—a starting point from which to work toward longer-term, more cohesive, more sustained professional development, including perhaps the creation of professional learning communities.

The six developmental stages we have described can be summarized as follows:

1. Articulating the curriculum

2. Implementing the curriculum

3. Incorporating effective instructional practices

4. Providing timely, targeted feedback

5. Establishing professional learning communities

6. Fostering professional development

Mathematics leaders should carefully consider each of these stages, viewing the developmental nature of the stages as well as the embedded continuous-improvement process. Successful work at one stage should positively influence work in other stages, and the next stage in particular.

All of the stages are headlined by the major leadership goal of engaging and empowering staff members.

LOOPING, OR RECYCLING, THROUGH THE DEVELOPMENTAL STAGES

An honest critique at each stage should be part of the developmental process. Mathematics leaders do not have to rely on their own judgment; they can gather evidence and opinions from teachers and administrators. Careful analysis and review are important to assess the effectiveness of each stage.

Continuous improvement will mean looping, or recycling, through the stages multiple times. Once the developmental stages have been implemented initially, a new cycle may need to start at a different point. This decision should be based on an overall critique. It is appropriate to loop back to any stage, if the evidence exists to support such a decision. Again, we would remind readers that the order of the stages is intentional but not rigid. For example, the developmental stage of articulating the curriculum (Stage 1) may have been well accomplished, while more work may be needed on implementing that curriculum (Stage 2). Therefore, mathematics leaders need not lead teachers through Stage 1 again. Rather an appropriate second starting point for a loop will be Stage 2.

Similarly, a comprehensive critique may show that, although moving through the developmental stages in order, one or more stages can be skipped or given only slight attention in a subsequent cycle. Others may need another full-scale treatment. Again, a thorough, careful critique will be the key to making decisions about the extent of treatment each stage should be given and whether some stages can be omitted from subsequent cycles.

MATHEMATICS LEADERS' INFLUENCE

Effective mathematics leaders can exert substantial influence over teaching and learning, just as effective mathematics teachers significantly influence student learning. The extent of leaders' influence will be directly related to positive actions that increase student learning. Student achievement, especially as it decreases the achievement gap and produces true equity, is the bottom line. Just as teachers engage students with effective strategies that increase what and how they learn, so must leaders engage teachers with effective strategies that help teachers acquire and use new or improved instructional methods fully aligned to the intended curriculum. Engagement and empowerment must ripple throughout the change process in order to produce the desired results.

Throughout this book we have emphasized the vital need for strong coherence among the intended, implemented, and attained curricula. It should always be borne in mind that the intended mathematics curriculum is the foundation required for successful planning and delivery of lessons. A successful mathematics curriculum will be one that is developed under the guidance of mathematics leaders who ensure that teachers have access to content standards and understand them. A direct result should be lessons planned to curricular specifications accompanied by intended resource materials—and then delivered as planned, using well-thought-out, effective instructional strategies. All of these elements of success will—or should—bear the stamp of effective mathematics leaders.

Such coherence will not happen by accident. Reflective practice is the process that can ensure such an outcome. When mathematics leaders and teachers base what they do on targeted, organized data about which they have thought deeply and that they have discussed thoroughly, then coherence can be better accomplished. Mathematics leaders control data management. Thus, effective development of coherence will depend largely on how well leaders collect, organize, report, and share pertinent data to inform and shape the collective work of leaders, teachers, and other stakeholders in the improvement initiative.

Finally, we would also reiterate that professional development must be targeted to the needs of classroom teachers as they work to close the achievement gap and improve overall student learning. Mathematics leaders most productively influence professional development content and style of delivery by asking teachers for input, observing teachers' and students' needs, and planning professional development accordingly.

We know that collegiality and professionalism among teachers also help to increase student learning. These characteristics do not occur naturally in very many schools. Teachers often work—indeed, may be expected to work—in relative isolation. Mathematics leaders can and should alter this norm by building collaborative relationships and professional teams. Establishing professional learning communities enables stakeholders to discuss teaching strategies and create lessons that truly improve student learning.

Closing the achievement gap and attaining equity in mathematics education for all students are formidable challenges. As a mathematics leader, you can meet those challenges by engaging and empowering your staff in working through the stages presented.

GUIDING QUESTIONS FOR CRITIQUING THE DEVELOPMENTAL STAGES

We conclude this book with a series of questions intended to help mathematics leaders and teachers examine their work in the developmental stages of the model we have described. These are reflection questions. Mathematics leaders may adapt them or add to them so that the critique best suits their school or district. The optimum result is a positive response to each question.

Ensuring an Articulated Curriculum

- Does your district have a clearly articulated scope, sequence, and timeline organized, at minimum, in six- or nine-week sections?
- Are the scope and sequence aligned to state and local standards (not the textbook)?
- Is the document easy to read, understand, and use; does it have sufficient specificity?
- Are there recommended instructional strategies in the document?

- Do the suggested materials align to state or local standards?
- Are effective instructional strategies included in district materials?

Ensuring an Implemented Curriculum

- Are teachers using the curriculum document?
- Are benchmark assessments administered in the district?
- Are the benchmark assessments administered at least every six or nine weeks?
- Do district-level administrators review assessment data?
- Are district and school achievement data analyzed?
- Are classroom visits occurring?

Using Effective Practices

- Is there evidence that professional development strategies are being implemented?
- Do teachers use a variety of instructional practices?
- Do materials reflect and support desired strategies?
- Are data used to inform instructional practices?
- Is research on learning identified and translated into teachers' actions?

Providing Timely Feedback

- Do mathematics leaders (including principals) frequently visit classrooms with a specified purpose?
- Are classroom visits for support, not evaluation?
- Do leaders compile trend data from the visits?
- Is there evidence that scope, sequence, and timeline are being used?
- Are data gathered about learning objectives and instructional strategies?
- Are data or information adequately shared with appropriate staff?
- Do instructional leaders continually meet with teachers in a variety of contexts to provide adequate feedback?
- Are classroom and school scores accrued, analyzed, and charted by student subgroup?

Facilitating Professional Learning Communities

- Do teachers have adequate time to meet?
- Are teachers discussing the district curriculum documents?
- Are teachers sharing effective instructional strategies?
- Are teachers planning common lessons?

- Do teachers have collaborative time to reflect on lesson results?
- Are assessment data being used to highlight effective strategies?
- Are teachers meeting to discuss lesson outcomes?
- Are teachers analyzing and studying student work?
- Are teachers using information to plan future lessons?

Requiring Professional Development

- Are teachers receiving help in changing classroom practices?
- Are professional development activities a reflection of the needs identified by classroom visits and collegial conversations?
- Are strategies reflected in data gathered by classroom visits?
- Are strategies embedded in the curriculum document?

References

Achieve. (2004). *Ready or not: Creating a high school diploma that counts.* Washington, DC: Author.

Achieve. (2006). *Closing the expectations gap: An annual 50-state progress report on the alignment of high school policies with the demands of college and work.* Washington, DC: Author.

Adelman, C. (2006). *The toolbox revisited: Paths to degree completion from high school through college.* Washington, DC: U.S. Department of Education.

Aschbacher, P. (1991). Performance assessment: State activity, interest, and concerns. *Applied Measurement in Education, 4,* 275–288.

Ashton, P. (1984). Teacher efficacy: A motivational paradigm for effective teacher education. *Journal of Teacher Education, 35*(5), 28–32.

Balka, D. (2002). *Exploring geometry with Geofix.* Rowley, MA: Didax.

Ball, D. L., & Wilcox, S. L. (1989). *Inservice teacher education in mathematics: Examining the interaction of context and content* (RR 89–3). East Lansing: Michigan State University, National Center for Research on Teacher Education.

Bell, A., Greer, B., Mangan, C., & Grimison, L. (1989). Children's performance on multiplicative word problems: Elements of a descriptive theory. *Journal for Research in Mathematics Education, 20*(5), 434–449.

Bergeron, J., & Herscovics, N. (1990). Psychological aspects of learning early arithmetic. In P. Nesher & J. Kilpatrick (Eds.), *Mathematics and cognition* (pp. 31–52). Cambridge, UK: Cambridge University Press.

Bezuk, N., & Bieck, M. (1993). Current research on rational numbers and common fractions: Summary and implications for teachers. In D. Owens (Ed.), *Research ideas for the classroom: Middle grades mathematics* (pp. 118–136). New York: Macmillan.

Bishop, A. (1985). The social construction of meaning: A significant development for mathematics education. *For the Learning of Mathematics, 5,* 24–28.

Boaler, J. (2006). Urban success: A multidimensional mathematics approach with equitable outcomes. *Phi Delta Kappan, 87*(5), 364–369.

Brown, S., & Walter, M. (1983). *The art of problem posing.* Philadelphia: Franklin Institute Press.

Brown, S., & Walter, M. (1993). *Problem posing: Reflections and applications.* Hillsdale, NJ: Lawrence Erlbaum.

California Department of Education. (2007). Criteria for evaluating mathematics instructional materials. In *California evaluation criteria* (p. 4). Sacramento: Author.

Charles A. Dana Center. (2008). *What should I look for in a math classroom?* Retrieved August 19, 2008, from www.utdanacenter.org/mathtoolkit/support/look.php

Conzemius, A., & O'Neill, J. (2001). *Building shared responsibility for student learning.* Alexandria, VA: Association for Supervision and Curriculum Development.

Covey, S. (1991). *Principle-centered leadership.* New York: Summit.

Daggett, W. R. (2008). *Rigor/relevance framework™.* Retrieved March 13, 2009, from www.leadered.com/rrr.html

D'Ambrosio, B. (1995). Highlighting the humanistic dimensions of mathematics through classroom discourse. *Mathematics Teacher, 88,* 770–772.

Driscoll, M. (1983). *Research within reach: Secondary school mathematics.* Reston, VA: National Council of Teachers of Mathematics.

DuFour, R. (2004). The best staff development is in the workplace, not in a workshop. *Journal of Staff Development, 25*(2), 63–64.

DuFour, R., DuFour, R., Eaker, R., & Karhanek, G. (2004). *Whatever it takes: How professional learning communities respond when kids don't learn.* Bloomington, IN: National Educational Service.

Dukewits, P., & Gowin, L. (1996). Creating successful collaborative teams. *Journal of Staff Development, 17*(4), 12–15.

English, F. (2000). *Deciding what to teach and test.* Thousand Oaks, CA: Corwin.

English, L., & Halford, G. (1995). *Mathematics education: Models and processes.* Mahwah, NJ: Lawrence Erlbaum.

Fullan, M. (1993). *Change forces.* London: Falmer.

Fuson, K. (1986). Roles of representation and verbalization in the teaching of multi-digit addition and subtraction. *European Journal of Psychology of Education, 1,* 35–56.

Fuson, K., & Briars, D. (1990). Using a base-ten blocks learning/teaching approach for first and second grade place-value and multi-digit addition and subtraction. *Journal for Research in Mathematics Education, 5*(21), 180–206.

Garmston, R., & Wellman, B. (1999). *The adaptive school: A sourcebook for developing collaborative groups.* Norwood, MA: Christopher-Gordon.

Hall, G., & Hord, S. (2001). *Implementing change: Patterns, principles, and potholes.* Needham Heights, MA: Allyn & Bacon.

Hiebert, J. (1988). A theory of developing competence with mathematical symbols. *Educational Studies in Mathematics, 19,* 333–355.

Hiebert, J., & Carpenter, T. (1992). Learning and teaching with understanding. In D. Grouws (Ed.), *Handbook of research on mathematics teaching and learning* (pp. 65–97). New York: Macmillan.

Hoachlander, G., Alt, M., & Beltranena, R. (2001). *Leading school improvement: What research says.* Berkley, CA: Southern Regional Education Board.

Hope, J., & Owens, D. (1987). An analysis of the difficulty of learning fractions. *Focus on Learning Problems in Mathematics, 9*(4), 25–40.

Huitt, W. (2000). Teacher efficacy. Retrieved May 17, 2005, from chiron.valdosta.edu/whuitt/col/teacher/tcheff.html

Hull, T., Balka, D., & Harbin Miles, R. (2009). *A guide to mathematics coaching.* Thousand Oaks, CA: Corwin.

Iowa Department of Education. (2005). *Improving rigor and relevance in the high school curriculum.* Des Moines: Iowa Department of Education.

Jensen, E. (1998). *Teaching with the brain in mind.* Alexandria, VA: Association of Supervision and Curriculum Development.

Johnson, J. (2000), *Teaching and learning mathematics: Using research to shift from the "yesterday" mind to the "tomorrow" mind*. Olympia: Washington State Office of Superintendent of Public Instruction.

Kanold, T. (2005, July 19–22). *The flywheel effect of a professional learning community*. Presentation at NCSM Leadership Academy, Park City, UT.

Kaser, J., Mundry, S., Stiles, K., & Loucks-Horsley, S. (2001). *Leading every day: 124 actions for effective leadership*. Thousand Oaks, CA: Corwin.

Kennedy, M. (2005). *Inside teaching: How classroom life undermines reform*. Cambridge, MA: Harvard University Press.

Lampert, M. (1992). Teaching and learning long division for understanding in school. In G. Leinhardt, R. Putnam, & R. Hattrup (Eds.), *Analysis of arithmetic for mathematics teaching* (pp. 221–278). Hillsdale, NJ: Lawrence Erlbaum.

Little, J. (1982). Norms of collegiality and experimentation: Workplace conditions of school success. *American Educational Research Journal, 19*, 325–340.

Loucks-Horsley, S., Love, N., Stiles, K., Mundry, S., & Hewson, P. (2003). *Designing professional development for teachers of science and mathematics*. Thousand Oaks, CA: Corwin.

Love, N. (2002). *Using data/getting results: A practical guide for school improvement in mathematics and science*. Norwood, MA: Christopher-Gordon.

Mack, N. (1993). Learning rational numbers with understanding: Building on informal knowledge. In T. Carpenter, E. Fennema, & T. Romberg (Eds.), *Rational numbers: An integration of research* (pp. 85–105). Hillsdale, NJ: Lawrence Erlbaum.

Marzano, R. (2001). *Classroom instruction that works: Research-based strategies for increasing student achievement*. Alexandria, VA: Association for Supervision and Curriculum Development.

Marzano, R. (2003). *What works in schools: Translating research into action*. Alexandria, VA: Association for Supervision and Curriculum Development.

Marzano, R., Walters, T., & McNulty, B. (2005). *School leadership that works: From research to results*. Alexandria, VA: Association for Supervision and Curriculum Development.

Mason, J. (1987). What do symbols represent? In C. Janvier (Ed.), *Problems of representation in the teaching and learning of mathematics* (pp. 73–81). Hillsdale, NJ: Lawrence Erlbaum.

McKean, E. (Ed.). (2005). *New Oxford American dictionary* (2nd ed.). MA: Oxford University Press.

Monroe, E. E., & Panchyshyn, R. (1989, April-May). *Success in mathematics: The vocabulary connection*. Paper presented at the annual meeting of the International Reading Association, New Orleans, LA, April 30–May 4.

National Commission on Education. (1983). *A nation at risk*. Washington, DC: Government Printing Office.

National Commission on Mathematics and Science Teaching for the 21st Century. (2000). *Before it's too late: A report to the nation from the national commission on mathematics and science teaching for the 21st century*. Washington, DC: U.S. Department of Education.

National Council of Supervisors of Mathematics. (2008). *PRIME leadership framework: Principles and indicators for mathematics leaders*. Bloomington, IN: Solution Tree.

National Council of Teachers of Mathematics. (2000). *Principles and standards for school mathematics*. Reston, VA: Author.

National Council of Teachers of Mathematics. (2006). *NCTM curriculum focal points*. Reston, VA: Author.

National Council of Teachers of Mathematics. (2008). *Equity in mathematics education* (position statement). Retrieved March 2, 2009, from www.nctm.org/about/content. aspx?id=13490

National Mathematics Advisory Panel. (2008). *Foundations for success: The final report of the national mathematics advisory panel*. Washington, DC: U.S. Department of Education.

National Research Council. (1999). *Improving student learning: A strategic plan for education research and its utilization*. Washington, DC: National Academy Press.

National Research Council. (2000). *How people learn: Brain, mind, experience, and school*. Washington, DC: National Academy Press.

National Research Council. (2001). *Adding it up: Helping children learn mathematics*. Washington, DC: National Academy Press.

National Research Council. (2002). *Helping children learn mathematics*. Washington, DC: National Academy Press.

National Research Council. (2005). *How students learn: History, mathematics, and science in the classroom*. Washington, DC: National Academy Press.

Oxford, R. (1990). *Language learning strategies: What every teacher should know*. New York: Newbury House.

Reeves, D. (2004). *Accountability for learning: How teachers and school leaders can take charge*. Alexandria, VA: Association for Supervision and Curriculum Development.

Reeves, D. (2006). *The learning leader: How to focus school improvement for better results*. Alexandria, VA: Association for Supervision and Curriculum Development.

Reys, R., Lindquist, M., Lambdin, D., Suydam, M., & Smith, N. (2003). *Helping children learn mathematics*. New York: John Wiley.

Rose, B. (1989). Writing and mathematics: Theory and practice. In P. Connolly & T. Vilardi (Eds.). *Writing to learn mathematics and science* (pp. 15–30). New York: Teachers College Press.

Rosenshine, B., & Furst, N. (1971). Research in teacher performance criteria. In B. Smith (Ed.), *Symposium on research in teacher education* (pp. 27–72). Englewood Cliffs, NJ: Prentice-Hall.

Schmoker, M. (1999). *Results: The key to continuous school improvement*. Alexandria, VA: Association for Supervision and Curriculum Development.

Schmoker, M. (2004). Tipping point: From feckless reform to substantive instructional improvement. *Phi Delta Kappan, 2*, 424–432.

Schoenfeld, A., & Arcavi, A. (1988). On the meaning of variable. *Mathematics Teacher, 81*, 420–442.

Senge, P., Cambron-McCabe, N., Lucas, T., Smith, B., Dutton, J., & Kleiner, A. (2000). *Schools that learn: A fifth discipline fieldbook for educators, parents, and everyone who cares about education*. New York: Doubleday.

Shelton, M. (1985). Geometry, spatial development, and computers: Young children and triangle concept development. In S. Damarin & M. Shelton (Eds.), *Proceedings of the seventh annual meeting of the North American branch of the International Group for the Psychology of Mathematics Education* (pp. 256–261). Columbus: Ohio State University.

Short, P. M., & Greer, J. T. (2002). *Leadership in empowered schools: Themes from innovative efforts*. Columbus, OH: Merrill Prentice Hall.

Short, P. M., & Rinehart, J. S. (1992). School participant empowerment scale. *Educational and Psychological Measurement, 52*, 951–960.

Sowell, E. (1989). Effects of manipulative materials in mathematics instruction. *Journal for Research in Mathematics Education, 20*(5), 498–505.

Spillane, J., Diamond, J., Burch, P., Hallett, T., Jita, L., & Zoltners, J. (2002). Managing in the middle: School leaders and the enactment of accountability policy. *Educational Policy, 16*(5), 731–762.

Starnes, B. A. (2006). What we don't know can hurt them: White teachers, Indian children. *Phi Delta Kappan, 87*(5), 364–369.

Stronge, J. (2007). *Qualities of effective teachers.* Alexandria, VA: Association for Supervision and Curriculum Development.

Thompson, S. (2003). Creating a high-performance school system. *Phi Delta Kappan, 85*(3), 489–495.

Threadgill-Sowder, J. (1984). Computational estimation procedures of school children. *Journal of Educational Research, 77*(6), 332–336.

Tikunoff, W., Berliner, D., & Rist, R. (1975). *An ethnographic study of the forty classrooms of the beginning teacher evaluation study known sample* (Tech. Report 75–10–5). San Francisco, CA: Far West Laboratory.

Tye, K. A., & Tye, B. B. (1984). Teacher isolation and school reform. *Phi Delta Kappan, 65*(5), 319–322.

Van Oers, B. (1996). Learning mathematics as a meaningful activity. In L. Steffe & P. Nesher (Eds.), *Theories of mathematical learning* (pp. 91–110). Mahwah, NJ: Lawrence Erlbaum.

Wagner, S. (Ed.). (2005). *Prompt intervention in mathematics education.* Columbus: Ohio Resource Center for Mathematics, Science, and Reading.

Williams, B. (1996). *Closing the achievement gap: A vision for changing beliefs and practices.* Alexandria, VA: Association for Supervision and Curriculum Development.

Yackel, E., Cobb, P., Wood, T., Wheatley, G. & Merkel, G. (1990). The importance of social interaction in children's construction of mathematical knowledge. In T. Cooney (Ed.), *Teaching and learning mathematics in the 1990s* (pp. 12–21). Reston, VA: National Council of Teacher of Mathematics.

York-Barr, J., Sommers, W., Ghere, G., & Montie, J. (2001). *Reflective practice to improve schools: An action guide for educators.* Thousand Oaks, CA: Corwin.

Youngs, P., & King, M. (2002). Principal leadership for professional development to build school capacity. *Educational Administration Quarterly, 38*(5), 643–670.

Zepeda, S. (2004). *Instructional leadership for school improvement.* Larchmont, NJ: Eye on Education.

Index